COMEBACK KID

101 SHORT STORIES, ESSAYS, AND INSIGHTS TO IMPROVE COMMUNICATION SKILLS

TABLE OF CONTENTS

Author's Preface

The hardest time to go through a tough time is when you're going through it.

But what about after you are done going through it?

How do you feel then?

I don't know about you, but I feel proud.

I think:

'I went through this and came out stronger.'

I didn't know if others felt the same way.

Until one day, I realized that many people felt the same way.

The feeling of joy after pain.

There was this one manager I had a while back.

His name was Ed.

He terrified the workers on the floor.

A towering New Yorker, a brash man, and would say whatever was on his mind.

He had a lot of power.

He had the other senior managers quaking in their boots.

What was strange about Ed was that he would never yell at me.

Stuff that he'd rip into the other workers for were stuff that he'd let me slide on.

I thought it was because I was a young buck in the company.

He probably didn't want to hurt my confidence.

One day, Ed called me into his office for forgetting to do the time sheets.

I went into the office getting ready to be scolded.
He was like:
'Hey bud, you missed your time sheets.'

I responded with:
'My bad Ed, I will do them right away.'

As I got up to leave, I felt a bit bold.
I thought it would be wise to ask Ed about his personal life.
Which I did.
'Hey Ed, how's life been in Florida vs up north?'

This innocent question opened up endless conversation material.
Ed and I ended up talking in the office that day for **2 hours.**
At one point, I was like:
'I need to get back to my desk because my manager will wonder where I am.'

Ed pinged my manager and said:
'Hey, Armani will be with me for a few.'

My manager quickly responded back with:
'Yes sir.'

We continued to talk.
I heard his story.

I heard about how he started his first business as a 20-year-old.
He tried selling computer hardware when the internet was first becoming a thing.

He talked about his marriage.

His family troubles.

Ed's son hated him because of the move from up north to down south.

Because his son's girlfriend didn't want to do long distance...

The stories continued.

I noticed at the end of each story, Ed would close the loop.

He'd spot the lesson.

'Yes, my first business failed, but here's what I learned.'

'Yes, my son hates me now. But one day, he'll see that the move was for the greater good.'

Some may say that Ed was rationalizing.

But I saw a man who was advanced at spotting the silver lining.

The scientific method starts off with observing the natural world.

Then gaps in understanding are spotted.

A hypothesis is created.

The hypothesis is tested.

Results are gathered.

The results are broken down to extract conclusions.

I was observing my surroundings.

I noticed that whenever I was going to networking events, I was boring the hell out of myself and the senior managers.

We were making small talk and stopping at small talk:

'Ah I see, how long did you say you were working in the company again?'

But after the conversation with Ed, I formulated a hypothesis:

- Powerful people hate talking about their success alone. They would much rather talk about the series of defeats that led to their success. They want to share their comeback story with you.

So, I tested out this hypothesis.

I went to a bunch of networking events.

And each time I spoke to people of power, I built some rapport with them first.

Didn't want to jump straight into their Ls.

After the rapport was built, that's when I would sneak in questions about their Ls.

'What was it like getting fired from your first internship?'

That's when I would see their eyes **LIGHT UP.**

They enthusiastically put their cheese cubes down and shared their story.

> ***Humans are not afraid of failing.***
> ***They are afraid of the uncertainty that comes with failing.***

The uncertainty is the lack of deadlines.

- When will it end?

This is why tough times are tough when we are going through it.

But here's a life law:

- Nothing in nature is permanent.

It's just a dance of up & down.

We often have a negative attitude towards this life law:

'Ah shucks…. I am going through an amazing moment now, but it will soon be shrouded in darkness.'

But very people perceive the opposite of that:

'No matter how dark times are right now, I know it will be sunny again...one day.'

Imagine how much FIRE a person will tackle the dark times with if they had the latter perspective as well?

The encounters with Ed and the other managers required me to refine my hypothesis.

It's not only people of power who love talking about their comeback...

It's people in general.

We have a deep driving desire to turn setbacks into comebacks.

To turn the pain into knowledge.

And to show that we are made of steel.

In the *Comeback Kid,* you will be given 101 short stories that cover a variety of topics that deal with emotional resilience, maturity, and seeing the silver lining in the darkest of circumstances.

The ArmaniTalks brand is centered on communication skills, so you will get insights that help you channel your emotions (the good, the bad, and the ugly) to become much more articulate!

It's not just about going through the ups & down.

Eventually, you need to be able to articulate your story into words.

This is how you build confidence with yourself.

And this is how you pass the wisdom forward.

– ARMANITALKS

WHAT ALL CREATIVE PEOPLE HAVE IN COMMON

There are a few quotes which make you view life in a different way.

One of those quotes for me was:
"Most people overestimate what they can do in a day and underestimate what they can do in a lifetime."

There have been different variations of that quote.
But the one I provided is my favorite.

The reason it is my favorite is because of the difference between "a day" & "a lifetime."

Other variations of the quote include 1 day to 10 years.
Some say, 1 month to 1 year.
I have also have seen twists which say 1 hour to 24 hours.

For me, the day to life time creates the biggest VOLTAGE.

'Voltage? We are talking about communication, not batteries.'
In some ways, we are talking about the same thing.

When a person buys something, they feel something.
Especially when it's not a mandatory item.

If it's a picture frame...they are feeling something in their body.
This feeling creates a pressure within them.

That's the language of the heart.
Pressure.

The difference between 2 things is what creates that pressure.
So two minus 1 is not that much of a difference.
Two trillion minus 1 creates a **sudden surge** in the body.

I open the email talking about this magical quote because I want
to reverse things for a second.

Rather than thinking in days or lifetimes...
I want to take away time.

Take away more time.
And a bit more...

'Why are you taking away all this time??'
Because that's what creative people have in common.

They are highly resourceful creatures.
They don't need much in order to build something.

What is one of the most precious things in this world?
'Uh... money!'
What do people with a lot of money consider one of the most
precious things in the world?
'Time.'

These wealthy people use their money to buy back time.
They understand how time trumps money.

-If you can strip away time, pressure is added.
-When pressure is added, feelings within the body spike.
-When feelings spike, either you panic, or you create like a mega
star.

Sure, we overestimate what we can do in a day.
But how much are we underestimating what we can do in 20
minutes?

If you are struggling with writer's block, shave away time.
If you are stuck on what to say for your next Zoom team meeting,
shave away time.
Have now clue how to deliver your brother's best man speech?

Shave away time...

Logically, you think that you'll sound like an idiot.
A part of you thinks:
'No, the crowd will hate me for it!'

Ironically, they will love you for it.

Sure, logically you think you'll sound like an idiot.
However, the illogical human will surprise you.

Shave away time, and personality starts to skyrocket.
You become funnier.
Simpler to understand.
And speak with a simple voice.

FEAR OF SPEAKING UP WHILE SITTING DOWN

When I first started the ArmaniTalks brand, I was giving away free 15 minutes consultation calls to get my practice off the ground.

This allowed me to see what people's pain points were and to see if we could work together in the future.

In the initial stages, I expected most of these people to come to me with the same issue.
Something along the lines of:

-speech anxiety for a best man speech.
-speech anxiety anxiety for a conference.
-speech anxiety while presenting at work.

All issues where they were standing UP in front of a crowd and speaking.
'Are you saying that wasn't the case?'
Yes, that's exactly what I'm saying.

Sure, some came to me with those fears that I listed above.
But an overwhelming amount contacted me about their fear of **speaking up while sitting down.**

Let's say you're at a team meeting.
Everyone is sitting & sharing their ideas.

But not you.
You feel resistance.

Others continue to speak.
While you remain quiet....
Why?

More on that shortly.

Or what about those moments when you are new to a work
environment, and someone says:

*'Alright guys, let's go around the room and say our names plus
a fun fact about ourselves. You can stay in your sits as you
speak.'*

I was getting hit with a bunch of calls from DIFFERENT parts of
the world....
Canada, Australia, India, Philippines.
With people telling me how much they feared speaking in a
group.

That's when I learned something:
-Public speaking means different things to different people.

I want to explain this issue very logically.
Remember this, you cannot conquer what you cannot verbalize or
articulate.

#1. Most people aren't often standing up and giving speeches.

If you are an average person out there, you may have a few
moments in your life when you are giving a speech in front of a
crowd.

I doubt you are giving a best man speech every other week.
Unless you are a very popular guy.

I doubt you are speaking at a conference every other week.
Unless you are a very popular guy.

'So?'
So, when you are having these special moments of speaking in
front of an audience, I'm sure **planning** is involved.

Planning helps you know what to say.
When you know what to say, a lot of the fear is reduced.

*While on the other hand, speaking up while sitting down can
happen every other week.*
A family meeting, work meeting, networking meeting etc.

Since it is happening so often, the TYPE of speaking is more impromptu, rather than planned style.
This is what scares a lot of people.
The fact that they have to think on their feet.

#2 Sitting can hurt body posture

When you're talking in front of a crowd, there is more alertness on your body.
Hopefully, your posture improves.

Plus, when you're standing up while others are sitting down, subconsciously, you feel higher valued.

On the other hand, while sitting, you meet someone eye to eye.
The higher valued narrative is removed.

Sitting can lead to more slouching.
Which makes it difficult to breathe.
Especially when you're nervous.

Add in the anxiety PLUS the variable of you impromptu speaking...
Now this fear makes a lot of sense.

'What advice did you give to these people who had this fear?'
First, I told them to articulate the issue from their own words.

This allows them to light fire into the darkness.
Self awareness can reduce fears.

More importantly, I told them to speed up, rather than wait up.

Remember this...
The people I was speaking with were from different parts of the world.
Canada, Australia, India etc.

However, they had this similar narrative which ran in their mind.
'Which was?'
That others were going to make it easy on them to speak.

A part of them assumed that others could tell when they wanted to speak.
So the others would eventually pipe down & there will be a large silence in the meeting.
That's when the quiet person could express their ideas with clarity & ferocity!

Imagine their shock when that never happened.

Instead, the conversation was a hurricane.
Going from 1 topic to the next to the next.

Which made the nervous person think:
'Let me wait for the perfect time.'

There is no perfect time bud.
Real world isn't like school.

-In school, you raise your hand and the teacher calls on you.
-In the real world, you raise your hand and call on yourself.

I told them that there would be BLIPS (short bursts) in the conversation where it was silent.
Not very long like their imagination made them think.

All good, blips are fine.
That was their opportunity to speak.

But don't just say something because there is a blip.
Say something if there is something worth saying.

Once they were priming their minds to look out for those blips of silences, that's when they decided they were going to speak.

'What if others cut them off?'
Then others would cut them off.

But the mere act of speaking in a blip builds 10000x more courage than just overthinking.
This courage has a spillover effect for the next meeting.
Where they would speak in another blip.

And so on...and so on....

The thing is, when they did speak up, the reaction was often positive.
Other members would nod their head and be like: *'interesting, I never thought of that.'*
Then other members would agree.

Those consulting calls taught me a lot about public speaking.
From speaking on stage, to speaking in a lowkey atmosphere.

FEAR OF SPEAKING OUT VS SPEAKING UP

There is a difference between the fear of speaking up vs the fear of speaking out.

'There is?'

Yes, there is.

The fear of speaking out is when an injustice was involved.

Let's say a local billionaire with a ton of influence turns a blind eye to discrimination happening in his local neighborhood.

At first, the other townspeople will not think much.

But later on, if the discrimination persists...

The townspeople will say:

'This fellow is afraid to **speak out** on the matter!'

While the fear of speaking up is normally due to self esteem issues.

Maybe being too shy, feeling inferior in social interactions, imposter syndrome, etc.

-The fear of speaking up is often a self imposed narrative.

-While the fear of speaking out is a narrative that is imposed by others.

Sometimes, I think whether these powerful people are even afraid to speak out.

Maybe their way of adding value is through a different way?

There are famous people who give silently rather than making a huge ruckus about it.

And if this group is not giving in the way that society expects them to give, then they will be labeled as a coward.

It's smart to understand the art of thinking for yourself.

That's the essence of communication skills.

The art of thinking for yourself comes down to getting data, understanding it & applying it for practical purposes.

Communication skills is the byproduct of knowing how to think.

Communication will be faulty when narratives are incorrectly cross applied.

Let's say this billionaire who is being labeled a coward by his own townsmen is not speaking up to the media.

However, he is making sure to work 1 on 1 with the people who are being discriminated against.

He is going out of his way to give them jobs.

One of the people being discriminated against recently lost his son in a motorcycle accident.

And this billionaire is paying for the entire funeral.

If we are viewing this fellow only from the lens of:

'Why didn't he speak out to the media??'

Then we would undermine the other positive things he did.

Priming the mind to think this way is difficult.

Especially in this era!!

This era rewards impulsiveness, fear mongering & regurgitating the same shit.

This is what I call the Rat Race for the mind.

That kind of content may get more noticed at first.

However, after consuming the content, it makes the mind more dependent.

-True knowledge should make you feel empowered & ready to take on the world.

-True knowledge should not make you feel oppressed & like a victim.

This is the key factor in determining whether you're learning or simply getting brainwashed.

So start learning the art of thinking if you are looking to improve your communication skills.

All the vocal exercises, singing to improve melody & body language will be much easier....

If you have something worth saying!

Communication skills done the right way should make you laugh at ever having felt fear to speak up.

Remember what I said about the fear of speaking up.

That's a **self imposed** narrative.

Fear of speaking up happens when the communicator puts the spotlight on them.

This fear is melted when the spotlight is placed on the idea.

All answers come back to thinking efficiently.

That's why I believe some form of content creation should be mandatory. Especially, in the information age.

View it like brushing your teeth.

You view it as obvious to take care of your teeth.

But you scoff at the notion of taking care of your mind..

Why?

'Uh...'

Exactly.

At least 10 minutes of creation a day keeps the limiting beliefs, propaganda & groupthink away.

KINGS, QUEENS, PRINCES & PRINCESSES

When I first started ArmaniTalks, I thought I was supposed to be the star of the show.

That must be the only way to get ideas on autopilot.

'Are you saying that was not the case?'
Correct.

I realized I was not the star of the show.

Instead, I was the sidekick.

'Who were you the sidekick to?'

The idea.

From 2018 to 2021, the transition has been:
Armani = King

Idea = Prince

To

Idea = King

Armani = Prince

Since the transition, it's easier to get ideas on autopilot.

And this isn't just for me, this paradigm flip has worked for my clients.

Most of my clients are men.

However, I've also had 2 women clients as well.

At the beginning of their journey, they felt a ton of nerves.

Fear of looking ugly when speaking, fear of judgment & fear of others things.

However, when they took up the role of the sidekick rather than the star...

They felt **free**.

For the longest, they were running a race with an anchor tied to their waist.

When they adopted the role of the prince or princess, rather than the king or queen, they got a metaphorical scissor to cut the rope which held the anchor!

After releasing the tension, ideas flew to them at rapid rates.

Rather than constantly worrying about how ugly they looked...

Now they enthusiastically redirected that mental energy to bring their idea to reality.

It took me 400+ YouTube videos, 330+ podcasts, 310+ blogs, 1,000+ emails, 4+ books and much more...

To realize it was never **fully** about me.

It was only **partially** about me.

I'm not of the philosophy of killing the ego.

I think it's much smarter to redirect the creative faculties of the ego to tell breathtaking stories on autopilot.

You may not have the time to practice as much as I have.

So try this instead...

Say out loud:

"I am the sidekick to my idea."

You'll feel strong physical sensations in your heart, legs, ears etc.

These physical sensations show you a new way of approaching communication skills....

POWER OF EDITING YOUR OWN WORK

There may come a day when I stop editing my own work.

All I do is create the ideas.

And outsource the proofreading, punctuation and spelling process.

Or maybe I keep it in house.

Who knows...

'Why would you keep that in house? Editing is the most boring part!'

You're right about that.

Well, that's what I used to think.

Editing was boring & a chore.

It's even more annoying when you **think** you caught all the mistakes, but that wasn't the case.

You ever watch those Masterclass commercials on YouTube?

They really know how to make a commercial.

Makes you want to check out what those classes are all about.

Recently, there was an Asian man who popped up on the ad.

He was a prodigy with playing the cello.

I watch the video all the way through.

Somewhere in the ad, he said something along the lines of:

'I had the audacity to think I could play the perfect note.'

He said he was once in a concert & everything was going perfectly well...

But he was bored out of his mind.

That night, he said he changed his paradigm.

He would dedicate the rest of his life to 'human expression' rather than 'human perfection.'

When I heard that, I resonated with it.

It's because there have been plenty of times when I was trying to perfectly edit a piece.

Whether it was a blog, email or tweet.

Only to notice that there was something that could have been done better.

I don't only mean in terms of spelling.

That happens.

That's something I'm okay with.

But I mean in terms of conveying the sentence.

When I read back my old writing, I see what **could have been** there rather than only trying to fix what was **already there.**

I realized the more that I edit my own writing, the more I began to think more efficiently as well.

It's because I built an internal compass to spot necessary vs unnecessary.

I think great writers are born in the editing process.

When they are getting a feel for what they like vs what they don't like.

A while back, editing was something I HAD to get rid of.

Nowadays, I do it with more joy.

Knowing that each rep that I put in, the more I am chasing human expression, rather than human perfection.

LEARNING EMOTIONS THROUGH ELECTRICITY

There are different parallels in life.

If you are astute and humble, you'll easily see the parallels.

While others look at you like a weirdo.

Before this month is up, I will be releasing a book on how to become a polymath.

This book will teach you how to learn better, study effectively & remain humble.

Humble gets a bad rep.

It's seen as being weak.

This is where we need to make our definitions clear.

Bad humble is when you compare yourself to people.

This will make you a nice guy in no time.

Good humble is when you compare yourself to the universe.

Or you can view yourself as a spec of sand in relation to a beach.

When you adopt this kind of humble attitude, you'll be able to perceive knowledge that others are not able to perceive.

Others often learn with the ego to prove how smart they are.

The modern-day polymath works with a higher purpose in mind.

Poor understanding of emotions leads to:

- A reactive attitude
- Excessive speech & social anxiety
- Inconsistency
- Low self-worth

Strong understanding of emotions leads to:

- A responsive attitude
- Speech & social confidence
- Consistency
- High self-worth

We will use electricity to understand emotions better.

I got my undergrad degree in electrical engineering and worked in different industries as an engineer.

Each time I learned more about electricity, each time I learned more about myself.

Here are some parallels.

1. Voltage = Embrace Every Emotion

It's dangerous to only have positive emotions towards positive emotions and negative emotions towards negative emotions.

It's better to have an equal eye towards both.

That's the recipe for greatness.

Become a human battery!

If you find a battery in your household, there will be a negative symbol and a positive symbol on it.

Without BOTH the negative & positive sides, the battery does not provide life to the circuit.

Your heart is like a battery.

It needs the negatives of fear, shame, anxiety etc.

It needs the positives of happiness, optimism, joy etc.

By accepting both emotions & using them for practical utility, you unlock the battery within.

That's emotional intelligence in a nutshell.

2. Electricity = Unity

Imagine your TV and lamp could talk.

One day, they are arguing with each another.

The TV calls the lamp skinny as a stick.

The lamp calls the TV fat as Pumba from Lion King.

They are about to fight.

That's when you come in and say:

'Chill guys! Y'all aren't as different as you think.'

They look at you confused and ask what you mean.

That's when you bring up how they are both able to function with **electricity**.

Now the lamp and TV don't only perceive the differences.

They perceive the unity first, then the differences.

This tiny mental flip leads to advanced judgment.

People are a lot like that too.

They have different bodies.

They have different minds.

Some are fat like a TV.

Some are skinny like a lamp.

But perceive them as having the same electricity.

This will make it easier to empathize.

3. Closed Circuit = Purpose

All functioning circuits have a closed loop.

Which implies that you allow the electricity to fully flow through a conductor.

If you cut the wire, then the electricity will stop flowing.

A conductor is something that allows for the flow of electrons.

Flowing electrons equals electricity.

If the conductor is just lying there, not connected to anything, then the electrons move around aimlessly.

Not producing any useful value.

But if you connect that conductor with a battery, switch, and a light bulb...everything changes.

The aimless electrons will flow through the circuit in one direction producing useful value.

Thoughts are electrons.

Most people's minds are aimless.

No direction or anything.

-They do what others tell them to do.

-They think what the media tells them to think.

-And they talk a bunch of shit.

But winners are different.

They connect the conductor to a lightbulb (their purpose).

They close the loop (commit).

They turn the switch on (are consistent).

All the electrons flow in 1 direction.

All the thoughts flow in 1 direction..

They are no longer aimless...

Realize this:

"Emotion" is a word created by humans.

Go past the word level and emotions become energy.

Just like electricity.

Show me a person who *can't* control their energy, and I'll show you a mess in the making.

Show me a person who *can* control their energy, and I'll show you a legend in the making.

DANGER OF ASKING THE WRONG QUESTIONS

I stumbled across a YouTube short recently that intrigued me.

There was a black guy who was calling into a show with a black host.

The caller was like:

'It feels like I'm surround by people who hate on me. I speak very proper. But my close friends say I talk like a white guy. How can I get them to accept me?'

The black host was like...

'You need to watch who you hang out with.'

Then the host gave the caller a lesson about asking the wrong questions.

If this caller went ahead and answered the question:

'How can I get others to accept my proper speaking?'

Would he have gotten an answer?
Sure.

But why even bother with the answer?
That time could have been spent doing other activities.

I'm sure you have heard the advice of distancing from toxic people.
Did you ever think about why?

Do toxic people only say statements that drain you?

Not always.

Some may put you down with statements.

But a lot of them ask draining questions which **force** a draining response out of you.

The questions that empower you deal with concepts, not with the opinions of others.

A conceptional question is:

'How can I be even more well-spoken?'

This question will lead you to reading more, writing more, and speaking with eloquent people about ideas.

A draining question is:

'How can I get other people to accept me?'

This question will lead you to dumbing yourself down and feeling empty inside.

Take time and evaluate the questions you ask.

Because questions influence answers.

Answers influence thoughts.

Thoughts influence behavior.

And behavior determines destiny.

PERMISSIONED VS PERMISSION-LESS LEVERAGE

A while back, there was an angel investor on Twitter named Naval who broke down how to get wealthy.

He talked about the different types of leverages out there.

He broke it down to:

-Permissioned and Permission-less leverage.

Even if you are not trying to get wealthy, I believe the concept of permission vs permission-less leverage sheds insight into the importance of people and technology.

I'd like share what I consider to be of paramount importance for both types of leverage.

First, let's talk about permissioned leverage.
Aka: *capital and labor.*

For capital, imagine that you are an entrepreneur in Silicon Valley.
You have an idea!

The problem?
You don't have any money!

So, you have to raise money.
You find a bunch of investors and share why your company will one day be valuable.
They give you money.

When the money is raised, you have the leverage to hire people, invest in equipment, invest in marketing etc.

The other form of permissioned leverage is labor.
This is when you have people working for you.

I know this girl named Ashely who owns a car repair company.
I believe she reads this newsletter, so shout out to you Ashley.

A while back, I had a flat tire.
I called Ashely.

She was like:
'I'll send my people to take care of that.'

Your people? I thought.
Then she sent her people.

There was a driver who came in this big car that had Ashely's company's logo on it.
Then another person from the passenger seat got out and fixed my tire.

Ashley had labor.
She had people who would follow instructions.

It's called permissioned leverage because:
-To get capital, someone has to give it to you.
-To command labor, someone has to follow you.

Now off to permission-less leverage.
Permission-less comes down to code and media.

Code is software that provides a service.
One great code is Hype fury.
It's a way to automate your tweets.

I use it and know the founder too.
Samy, cool dude.

He wrote a piece of code that provides value to others.
This code can be replicated fairly easily and allows his business to scale.

It's permission-less because no one told him what to code.
He just needed his laptop to get started.

The next kind of permission-less leverage is media.
We need to be more specific....
What type of media?

Am I talking about tv, radio, and newspapers?
Nah.

I'm talking about new media.
YouTube, podcast, and blogs.

Make a YouTube video once, and it'll be there forever.
I saw this in action from Vlad, the founder of Vlad Tv.

Vlad shares hip hop news.

He doesn't get much respect in the hip hop circle.

They view him as an undercover agent.

But what fascinated me about Vlad is that he has an engineer's mind.

It's because he was an engineer.

He thinks in processes and systems.

Brick by brick, he grew Vlad Tv.

Nowadays, he has a content empire.

You don't make riches from the video alone.

You make riches from the video **catalog**.

Recently, Vlad talked about how he plans to one day drop 100 clips a day.

That's a staggering amount!

And he doesn't need to get permission from anyone.

Permission and permission-less leverage do not always exist separately.

You can combine the 2.

For example:

An author who is self-published.

He has the permission-less leverage of media (books).

Also, he has the permissioned leverage of labor to create his cover designs and proofread the book.

Another example:

A seasoned realtor who has interns showing properties to potential customers.

That interns are labor.

Permissioned.

While the seasoned realtor focuses on answering common real estate questions on his blog.

Creating content on the blog is permission-less.

For permissioned leverage, communication skills are key.

You need crystal clear communication if you are asking someone for money.

And you need crystal clear communication if you plan to lead anyone.

With permission-less leverage, communication skills are also important.

But what's even more important is **DESIRE**.

Desire, because no one is hand holding you with permission-less leverage.

You are free to do whatever.

Granted that you don't get kicked off the platform.

This desire leads to commitment.

Commitment leads to creativity.

And creativity is the fuel to communication skills.

SHORT TERM THINKERS VS LONG TERM THINKERS

Twitter is a great platform.

But it's also a platform that shows the dark parts of people.

One dark part is the blatant plagiarism.

I don't mean getting the same concept of a tweet and rearranging the words.

I'm talking about copying a tweet word for word and posting it as your own.

Throughout the past couple of years, I have created 70,000+ tweets.

Every now and then, I go to the Twitter search section.

Type in a few of the key words from a past tweet and add 'armanitalks.'

That's when I'm presented with the full tweet.

For example, if I type in:

- Blossom, legend, just watch, armanitalks

That leads to the full tweet of:

- If you write it down, you will soon become it. Just watch. Journal who you want to become every day of your life. Force yourself to level up daily. Watch yourself blossom into a legend.

I always lose and gain new followers.

So posting some old school material gives new followers a chance to see my earlier stuff.

As I do this little exercise, I notice a bunch of people with my exact tweet!

Some tagged me at the end.

So that's not plagiarism.

That's called giving a shoutout.

But others don't have my named tagged.

It's my tweet being passed off as their own.

A lot of times, these are not big accounts.

200 followers or so.

Whatever.

But nowadays, I see bigger accounts doing this.

There was 1 account who had roughly 200,000 followers doing this.

Getting plagiarized is annoying.

But it's also good.

It's good because your material is worth plagiarizing.

Also, it keeps you motivated to sharpen your thinking faculties so no matter how much you get copied, you're **always** capable of coming out on top.

Walt Disney once said that he could innovate faster than his competitors could imitate.

Once Walt created his iconic Mickey Mouse character, there were all these other mouse characters popping up in cartoons.

Not too long after, Walt created Donald Duck.

His competitors were scrambling.

Getting plagiarized should light a fire under your ass and get you more creative.

Weird, I know

But it's true.

Another thing I noticed from this incident is the difference between short-term and long-term thinkers.

I believe when a long-term thinker looks at content, they see thinking processes.

That's all you're seeing right now.

My mind in word form.

So if content is my mind, solidified.

How can I consistently create content?

I know:

- Sharpen my mind!

A few years ago, I thought it would be smart to become smart.

Know a lot.

Connect ideas.

And keep practicing articulating ideas every day.

That's when I created an idea factory.

The ideas start off as a germ on twitter.

I expand on this newsletter.

YouTube, I create talks from inspiration.

Podcast, I too create talks from inspiration.

Tons of ideas and concepts to work with.

I compile the key ideas from the talks in a book format once my philosophy on a subject is solidified.

From there, rinse and repeat.

It's a **process**.

The engine of the ArmaniTalks business is to learn HOW to think.

The idea factory idea is of little interest to the short-term thinker.

They only think in week by week intervals.

Or worse, day by day intervals.

Their thinking faculties are dull.

They don't know how to see around the corners.

They thought they were being so smart by skipping the process.

But when you skip the process, the process finds you.

That's a life law.

Short term thinking is a lot like buying cheap clothes.

It feels good buying cheap clothes.

'Wow, I got such a great deal!'

But wait a few weeks....

Put those clothes in the washer and dryer.

And the clothes come out looking like trash.

Time does not favor low quality clothes.

Time does not favor short term thinkers.

THE GREATEST TEACHER ON THE PLANET

For us to know something in depth, we need 2 things:
-Intellectual understanding.
-Experiential understanding.

We may not always get both.
And even if we do get both, the 2 may not be equal in quantity.

But the better we optimize for both variables, the more we increase our chances of knowing a topic.

Intellect is the ability to reason.
Reasoning comes down to a bunch of:
-*"If this happens, this will happen,"* connections.

Example:
You're a little kid.
You see a person touch a hot stove.
The person immediately winces in pain.

The logical understanding is:
If someone touches a hot stove, then they will feel pain.

The mind only knows so much.
So, we don't do a logical analysis for everything.
We learn from reputable sources as well.

If your dad tells you:

'Hey John, don't touch the hot stove. You'll burn your hand.'

You will take the intellectual knowledge seriously.

The second is experiential knowledge.

This is when our breath and body goes through the process.

The little kid trusts their dad.

But they have a rebellious attitude.

They are like:

'I know my dad says I may burn my finger. But let me find out for myself.'

The kid touches the stove, feels the pain...

And now they have experiential knowledge as to why they shouldn't have touched it.

Btw, I'm not saying that you should touch a hot stove to see if it's really hot.

There are a lot of passive experiences that may have led you to that conclusion (where you pick up your hot plate too soon from the microwave).

And other times, the intellectual understanding is so strong, that an experiential understanding is not needed.

I don't need to kill someone to understand why it's bad.

Pursuing experiences comes down to intent, context, and judgment.

Although at times, we will be placed in situations beyond our control.

That's a talk for another time.

A storyteller combines the intellect and experience.

A storyteller shouldn't be a dummy.
-They should be smart enough to reason.

But a storyteller shouldn't be too smart.
-Because then they will use words that other people cannot experience.

If you can explain something intellectually with o experiential knowledge, then you may be too prideful.

You'll quote others and be like:
'I know these topics just as well as they do!'

And if you have experiential understanding, but cannot intellectually explain it overtime, then you'll think you were having a hallucination.
'Did that really happen or was it a dream?'

'How can I get a head start with being a better storyteller, Armani?'

First, get rid of the 'once upon a time' mentality.

When people think of stories, they think of:
'Once upon a time, there was a prince who rescued a princess from a dragon.'

Then they subconsciously view storytelling as impractical.

In my book, **<u>The Art and Science of Storytelling</u>**, I say that a story is:

-A series of ideas connected to provide value.

With that simple definition, we are capable of refining our movement.

Next, explain something you know very well.

Im talking very, very, verrryyyy well.

You know a topic very well if someone asked you to explain it, and you're like:

'Where do you want me to begin?!'

Once you have discovered a topic like that, use **at least** 1 analogy in your explanation.

'Why are analogies so important?'

Because analogies give other humans the illusion of experiential knowledge.

Imagine that someone never gave a speech before.

So they have no clue what speech anxiety is like.

Then I say:

*'Imagine how you feel at the peak of a roller coaster. Right before it's about to go down. Your heartbeat is getting faster and faster. Then you look down and see how high you are from the ground. The people on the bottom look like ants. You see how far the roller coaster is going to **plummet**. Your palms are sweating on that cold metal bar that's holding you back from your possible death. You feel that?'*

The listener nods.

'Well, imagine those same feelings before a speech. That same level of intensity is what speech anxiety is like.'

Although this listener never gave a speech, now they have something to relate to.

Recap:

If you want to become a better storyteller...

1. **Find a topic you know well enough to reason through.**

To find a topic like that, see if it passes the:

'Where do you want me to begin?!' test.

To better create this analogy, assume the listener has no clue what you're talking about.

Make it real for them.

By merging intellectual and experiential understanding, the storyteller becomes the greatest teacher on the planet.

EVERYTHING HAPPENS FOR A REASON

A few years ago, I was losing respect for the media.
Yellow journalism, clickbait headlines & outrage news on the daily.

It disgusted me!

I slowly began to look down on journalism.
What's the hype about them anyways?
They are the bottom feeders of society.

A few years later, around 2019, I ended up joining an organization called BNI.
This is a business networking group.

I met business men & women from all walks of life.
Met people in the car repair industry.
Lawn mowing business.
Yoga studio etc.

This was a great networking & learning opportunity.

As my first year was winding down, one day, I got a call from the upcoming president.
He said:
'Arman, I want you to be the Communications Chair for the upcoming term.'

Initially, I thought:
'Hm.. interesting. But I don't know if I can do it.'

I don't know why I doubted myself.
Probably because of time constraints.

But something in my gut told me to take it.
I was honored that the upcoming president directly contacted me.

I accepted.

I went to get trained for the new position in a Conference.
The Communication's Chair records the content of the meeting,
gathers announcements, sends out newsletters etc.

That conference was eye opening & I wanted to do the best job
that I could.

For the next few meetings, I made sure my phone was charged.
Also, I would bring a notepad & pencil.

I'd take pictures and make notes of the important moments of the
meeting.

Then every Friday, I compiled the information, created a story
newsletter & sent it out to the members of my club.

It was great hearing messages like:
'This newsletter is on point! It feels like I was at the meeting.'

That was my goal.

Business men & women are busy.
They cannot always make the meetings.
So I wanted my BNI newsletter to be detailed & fun to read so
others FELT like they were in attendance.

**I was doing something, but I didn't know what I was
doing.**

As I tried to find a word for what I was doing, I did some
research.
The process of getting information, processing information,
organizing information & communicating information is known
as:

JOURNALISM!!

That's when I was led back to my past.
A field that I was disgusted by was now a field that I was
unknowingly partaking in.

I decided to give this field another look with a less biased eye.
'How did you do that?'
I found some lectures on journalism & watched it.

There was an old man who taught the history of journalism, why the subject was important to society & best practices to deliver information.

The more I watched the lecture, the more he put words to my experiences.

My life as the Communications Chair for BNI suddenly intertwined with my past.

No longer was I disgusted by journalism.
I was now disgusted with the bad apples of journalism.

This also showed a flaw that anyone is prone to.
'Which is?'
Bias.

This moment of my life taught me the art of how to restrain myself from having an opinion.
And to look closely at fields that I detest.

Every field has bad apples.
In our era, journalists have some of the worst reputations out there.
Along with police officers.
And course creators.

When looking closer, ALL fields have negative stigmas & bad apples.
Limited minds use others to paint their narratives for them without doing further 'digging.'

Yes, that's a journalism phrase that I learned from the lecture.
Digging means to research further.

The Mega Minds make mental notes of the feeling of repulsion in their body.
But they don't immediately offer their 2 cents like they know the subject.

Instead, they do further research if the topic is important enough.
Or they say something like:
'I don't know enough on the topic to have an opinion.'

Everything happens for a reason.
But it takes a while to make the connections.

The connections sometimes present itself.
Where a mind that was not searching is like :
'Whoa, that moment from the past suddenly clicked.'

This is a suboptimal strategy.

It's much better to ACTIVELY look for connections.
Train your mind to be in connecting mode.
That's the purpose of writing & speaking.

When you actively find connections from the different stages of
your life, that's when you reach surreal insights that others could
never imagine.

Words not only allow you to express yourself.
Words also allow you to travel across time.

-Rewire your interpretation of the past.
-Give clarity to the present.
-And engineer a compelling vision for the future.

WALKING A MILE IN SOMEONE'S SHOES

I once read the book, To Kill a Mockingbird.

One of the important characters in the book is a man named Atticus Finch.

Atticus is a strait-laced lawyer who reads all the time.

The conflict in the story is when he is supposed to defend a black man who was accused of rape by a white woman.

The story was set during a time where racism was at an all-time high.

Atticus accepting a case like that was enough to make him a pariah in the community and within his family.

Atticus's 2 kids were Scout (girl) and Jem (boy).

They were getting made fun of by the other kids because their father was defending a black man.

A few times, Scout got into fights with others who insulted her father.

And routinely, Atticus would tell her to take the high road.

Atticus said:

'Scout, before you judge someone, I want you to try wearing their skin.'

Strange phrasing...

But it was a remix to the 'walk a mile in their shoes' quote.

With this type of empathy, it's easier to be patient and build more perspective as a byproduct.

Recently, I was on a road that I normally drive on.

That road has had more homeless people as of late.

Each homeless person has a sidewalk they claim as their own...

They ask for money there.

The road that I was on had a homeless man that was roughly 35 years old, white, and looked like he had been to hell and back.

Normally, he is very calm.

However, when I was driving on the road recently, something changed.

Whenever the lights turn red and all the cars are stopped, that's when this homeless man goes from car to car asking for money.

On this particular day, I could see a bunch of hands waving this person off.

He was getting closer to my car.

I don't carry cash like that; I normally have cards.

As he came to the car in front of me, he asked for money.

The hand shooed him away.

Rather than walking away.

The homeless man became **livid**.

He starts yelling at the driver.

And starts motioning his hand to his face like:

'I need food.'

He made this hand motion very aggressively.
Jabbing his hand to his face.

I could see from behind that the driver shrugged his shoulders.
He was with a younger woman, who I believe was his daughter.

Suddenly, the homeless man stood right in front of the car and began pounding it!!

I couldn't believe what I was seeing.
This homeless guy was normally so calm.
And now he was so angry.

I'm surprised the guy who was getting his car hit didn't get out and beat up the homeless guy.
I'm surprised no cops stopped the incident. That area is normally surrounded by undercover cops.

Rather than driving around the homeless guy, the driver just sat there.
There were cars driving on my right-hand side, so I couldn't leave either.
So, I had no option but watch this thing play out.

What would happen next?

The driver was muttering something to his daughter.
His daughter put her hand on the driver's shoulder and probably said something like:
'Just let him be angry.'

Or she may have said a quote like:
'Wear his skin for a few.'

The driver let the guy hit on his car.
The homeless guy eventually came back to sanity.
Then walked back to the sidewalk.
And the driver drove off.

I am not too sure what to make of this.
I don't know if I would have been so calm with someone hitting my car when I said I didn't have any pocket change.

Seeing the driver's composure bought out a composure in me for the rest of the day.
Later, I went to do grocery shopping and the lady who was at the cash register was very slow.
Rather than immediately getting angry, I maintained my cool.

I didn't have to **try** to maintain my cool either.
It just happened.

There are a lot of lessons from fiction books which are applicable to real life.
Not only that, but seeing someone else take the high road activates the mirror neurons in the brain for us to do the same.

There is a saying out there that talks about:
'You become the average of your 5 best friends.'

I believe in addition to that:

'You become the information you consume and the experiences you assign importance to.'

I assigned importance to the composure displayed by the driver that day.

Therefore, patience was a byproduct.

THE WORST PERSON TO COMPETE WITH

64

One of the most dangerous people to compete with is the person who doesn't compete with others.

I believe this mindset will become more valuable in the coming ages.

2 years ago, I went to this wedding and saw one of the funniest things.

This was a wedding where there were 2 best men.

Let's call them Ravi and JoJo.

Ravi constantly kept competing with JoJo.

Ravi was livid that the groom asked JoJo to be a best man too.

So, the wedding was a chance for Ravi to prove his dominance.

JoJo was aware of the competition that Ravi was waging, but didn't really care.

He was sitting at our table.

One of the guys from the table asked JoJo:

'Hey, are you aware that Ravi is looking to outshine you in the wedding?'

JoJo laughed and said:

'Yea, he's an idiot.'

When he waved off Ravi like that, I almost spit out my water.

Here was one guy who was waging a holy war.

And the other guy was just viewing him as a joke!

Ravi was first up to give a speech.

And his talk was phenomenal.

I believe Ravi had some Army training and was in charge of a lot of people.

Which gave him training on how to be well spoken.

By the time JoJo goes up, something strange began happening.

The cameramen wanted JoJo to stand still at the center of the stage while looking at the bride and groom when giving his talk.

Where Ravi was walking around freely on stage.

The cameramen were asking JoJo to stand still.

Not only that...

If he were to look at the bride and groom the entire time, then his back would be facing the audience!

Which is a public speaking no-no.

The cameramen were saying that they needed to set their cameras down, and their commands were mandatory.

I could slightly hear the conversation because I was in the front of the audience.

That's when JoJo did something...

He said, 'sure, I'll stand in the same spot the entire time.'

The cameramen smiled and walked off stage.

When the cameramen walked off stage, JoJo ripped the mic off the stand, and began walking around stage!

The audience erupted in applause by the blatant disrespect towards authority.

For the next 13 minutes, JoJo gave his speech.

I thought Ravi's talk was way better and more polished.

Ravi's talk was around 7 minutes, which I believe was the better length for a best man speech.

However, JoJo's speech was more emotional.

He talked about the ups and downs with the groom, talked about the bride, told some compelling stories, and wrapped up.

Once the speech was done, the audience clapped.

It seemed like the war had ended.

Actually, no...it didn't end.

Ravi was furious that JoJo had almost double the time as him.

Others in the wedding were now becoming aware of how Ravi had waged a war on JoJo, so they decided to tease him.

They jokingly said:

'Ravi, JoJo's speech was way better than yours!'

They had been drinking and felt like comedians.

Ravi didn't laugh.

He was getting furious with each joke.

The more furious he got, the more it was comedy gold for the drunk roasters!

As the night winded down, I observed JoJo and Ravi.

I saw how they were polar opposite of each other.

One guy was competing with someone who was not competing back.

Ironically, the guy who was not competing back was dominating.

Why??

It's because in creative fields, competition takes away focus from what really matters.

That's the product.

The product is the story.

A person who is dwelling on other humans will fall flat in the long term to the person who is dwelling on more story ideas.

It's always been like that.

It will always be like that.

Even in business, that's the case.

There are groups of people who always watch what others are doing.

Back in the days, they would wait in the parking lot, observing someone else's moves while their own store was in shambles.

In certain industries, the competitors would dive in the dumpsters of their rivals to steal their recipes.

All effort that is taken away from making their own house better.

To see how the creative person wins requires a long-term thinking approach.

When going from micro to macro, the person who doesn't compete with others often gets the last laugh.

Hey... the laws of creativity don't always follow logic!

So, if you ever find yourself in this type of scenario, you may want to ask yourself:
'Am I conducting myself like a JoJo or a Ravi?'

BECOME A MASTER WITH WORDS

One subject I hated in school was Language Arts.
Not only did I hate the subject, I hated the teachers who taught it.

One of my teacher's name was Ms. Boileau.
I think she was a French woman.

No one could pronounce her name.
So, she would say:
'It's like Swallow with a B.'

Ms. Boileau was annoying.
She would nitpick & focus on on the little things.
She was a grammar nazi, wanted to make sure you had neat handwriting & indented with the proper spacing.

Language arts was brutal growing up.
Nowadays, I see it as a coveted skillset.

'Why the change?'
It comes down to 2D and 3D.

What are words really?
Words are concepts that are meant to express human experiences.

The human experiences are 3D.
The words are 2D.

The reason I hated Ms. Boileau's class was because she had me focusing too much on the 2D.

I was learning about words.

How to structure them.

How to use punctuate and all of that.

But I wasn't learning about what those words were expressing!!

That's like making a sandwich.

You're getting the:

Nice bread.

Nice turkey.

Nice lettuce.

Then you never eat it.

Instead, you & a bunch of your buddies gather around and stare at the sandwich.

When one person comes to you and asks:

'Why aren't you eating the sandwich?'

The herd looks at the questioner with a pompous attitude and says:

'You don't eat a sandwich. You look at it.'

That's what it's like to focus on the words without focusing on the experiences.

Ironically, the best way to get better with words is by not focusing on the words.

Focus on the human experiences first.
Focus on the 3D!

A great writer is a great introspector.
From elegant thinking, elegant writing falls out.

It's the same with poetry.
Poetry comes from the vision first...
Then the words are just there to express the vision.

There are 4 pathways to enter Language Arts:
-Speaking
-Reading
-Listening
-Writing

Don't confuse these as separate entities.
They are all different parts of the same animal.
Sort of like each leg of the same elephant.

Master each leg by focusing on human experiences first.
Go where the emotions & imagery reside...

DANGERS OF GLORIFYING SOMEONE

72

The mind is meant to dwell on concepts.
Not people.

When you dwell on people, you become anxious or overbearing.
Dwell on concepts instead.

I recall I went to this event a few years back.
That's when I ran into a kid I hadn't seen in years.
I'll call him Timothy.

Timothy told me he had been staying updated with my life.
That's when I had just graduated from college and got a job at a good company.

In the event, he said:
'Armani, you're my role model.'

It felt good to hear that.
It felt bad to hear that.

For the rest of the event, I felt like I had to put on some kind of show for this kid.
To live up to the role model title.

I recall this was an event with a few familiar faces. So I expected to be getting loose & having fun.

But I was more tamed knowing someone was viewing me as a role model.

This was a memory from 7 plus years ago.

In 2019 ish, I had a buddy set up my YouTube studio.

He's roughly around my age & I think he was starting a YouTube channel at the time.

One day, he gave me an unusual compliment.

He said:

'I like how you wear normal clothes in your videos. You just seem like a normal guy.'

I didn't think about that.

I normally record these videos in an integration format.

Where I'm going about my day & then do some recording.

Therefore, it's not a special occasion.

When he said that, I noticed the process of taking the glitz and glam **out** of content.

That's where a lot of glorification can happen nowadays.

It's a 2 fold issue.

Group 1 wants to be glorified.

Group 2 is intellectually lazy & wants others to think for them.

Let's break down group 1 first.

This group will phrase themselves as having all the answers.

Then they will deliver their message.

They will give a system.

"Follow the system and you're good to go."

Most of their advice is black and white.

'Are these people bad?'

Some are, some are not.

Instead, it is group 2 who is too blame.

Group 2 does not like to think.

When someone lacks experience, all advice seems like good advice.

When group 2 glorifies someone's, they think:

'Well, why should I bother making any decisions? I can just follow the other person and blame them if it doesn't work out!'

Group 1 may be giving pretty well thought out advice.

However, group 2's laziness and misguided attitude towards glorification causes them to morph group 1 into an evil presence.

Here's the fix.

Quit glorifying humans.

Humans are flawed creatures.

They make mistakes & errors like anyone else.

'Geez, that's bad.'

No, that's liberating!

When you go in with the assumption that humans are flawed creatures, now you can appreciate their insights in depth.

Rather than viewing all their advice in black & white lens.

You can view it in gray lens.

I don't like the idea of having only 1 mentor.

That may work in some fields.

But overall, it seems like an industrial age concept to me.

In the information age, the world is your mentor.

To capitalize on this, view those mentors as flawed creatures first & insightful creatures second.

Learning becomes fun when you quit glorifying people.

Because let's say you agree with 10 things this glorified person says.

But the 11th thing goes against everything you stand for.
What then?

1. You violate your principles.
2. You second guess everything this deity has said..

No need.

The person who never glorifies others will take what works....and eliminate what doesn't.

Easy peasy lemon squeezy.

WALK IT LIKE YOU TALK IT

You ever seen someone who took their job very seriously...
And you couldn't help but make fun of them a little?

I used to be that guy.
Let me give you a scenario.

In the Tampa International airport, the roads are typically busy.
Especially, on the weekdays.

There have been a handful of times when I go to pick up a
friend...he is only 5 minutes away from meeting me at my car.

As I'm waiting, I get a patrol officer knocking on my window,
saying:
'You can't be waiting here, son. Either pay for parking or leave.'

I'm not trying to pay for parking when the guy I'm picking up is
only 5 minutes away.
And when the patrol officer is telling me to "leave", he's really
implying, *take a spin around the airport until my friend is
PHYSICALLY at the meetup location.*

Taking a spin around the airport takes at least 10-15 minutes in
traffic.
So, it's a lose-lose situation.

I hated those patrol officers back then.
Still hate being in that predicament.
However, nowadays, I came to respect them.

They take their jobs seriously.
I'd rather you take your job seriously rather than not take it
seriously enough.

There was this guy who DM'd me recently asking me to try out a
software that he created.
Not only did he DM me, but he also left video messages giving me
demo's of his software.

Initially, I didn't see his DMs.
So unfortunately, I didn't respond back to him for a couple of
months.

But recently, I saw the DMs and responded back.

He sent me more video messages talking about how his software
could benefit me.
He even showed me the demo while he was on my Twitter profile.

I could tell this guy cared.

To take it a level further, he was the CEO of the company.
Not just a salesman, or an intern.
Look at the founder of the company taking his job so seriously!
Much respect.

With information technology on the rise, business owners are
becoming the CEO, marketing team, product development team,
sales team and all that in one package.

Many companies are becoming atomized.

'What does this mean for me, Armani?'
It means the future is gearing everyone to be a leader.

There are tiers of leadership though.
Some will command more people.
While others will command just a few.

The key is to have leadership qualities being cultivated in your
genes.
Walk it like you talk it.
Actually care.
Don't just pretend to care.

In my new blog post, I give you 8 traits of a leader.
If you can even take one of these skillsets seriously, you'll be
emerging in the atomized world what we will live in.

Command respect, because you embody respect.

WHAT IS YOUR NARRATIVE?

There is a YouTube account I followed a while back who is very underrated.

He talks about business through the content marketing model.
A very modest guy.

He normally wears a baseball cap and does his videos from his living room.
Some of his videos are 10 minutes.
Other videos are up to 2 hours long.

He gives away a lot of practical strategies such as:
-Search engine optimization,
-How to set up a website,
-Optimizing an email campaign etc.

Overall, seems like a standup guy.
He's recorded 400+ videos over the past couple of years.

As I watched his videos, I noticed he consistently brings up a concept over and over again.
'I'm not like all the other fake guru's out there.'

It's one thing if he says it every now and then.
That's not the case though.
He repeats this sentiment many times...

He despises fake gurus.
His disgust towards these characters causes him to keep outputting more and more quality information.

Recently, he announced that he was taking a break from YouTube.
He said that within the past couple of years, he built a beautiful system that has made him financially free.

He finds it rewarding to know that his video's impacted so many people.

I couldn't tell if this was his final video or if he was just taking a break.
But what I do know was that he left one final message for....
You guessed it!
The fake guru's.

It doesn't take rocket science to see what this man's narrative is.
If I were to put it into words from his lens, I think he built his YouTube channel with the core philosophy of:

'I aim to provide quality information so people are not scammed by get rich quick schemes.'

I believe this was the narrative that propelled his actions.

Is a narrative like this wrong?
Not necessarily.
Because it led to consistent output at the end of the day.

A narrative like this can get draining over time though.
Because it's **dependent** on someone else.

It can lead to supreme creativity.
But that creativity always needs a crutch.
Like a rapper who can only rap when he's high.
This type of creativity leads to the likelihood of burnout.

Consistency is focus made solid.
It's hard to focus when the eyes are always on someone else's lane.

Overall, this YouTuber seemed like a pleasant personality. A kind of person you wouldn't mind being friends with.

But every now and then, when the topic of fake guru's would come up, you'd immediately see his demeanor change.
I wonder if he was scammed for a lot of money back in the days?

It's hard to be ambitious and a top performer for a long period without a narrative occupying the mind.

When reading a book, if you read a bunch of random chapters, then it won't make much sense.

Well, unless you're reading my new book, <u>Word Play</u>. Since this book is a collection of short stories, the chapters aren't connected.

If you are reading a regular book and just going from chapter to chapter, chance are you will stop reading.

Same with activities.
If you are just doing activity after activity, that's creating a jagged mentality.

It's the theme that fuels productivity.
The theme colors the life behind the movements.

With this creator, he chose a theme that was dependent upon others.
Can't deny his output though.
He provided more quality in that YouTube channel than a lot of colleges.

However, one line did stick out in the end of his video.
He talked about how he wasn't getting much love from the YouTube algorithm.

His channel is highly underrated.
He talked about how he hated it that these Fake Guru's were getting the love, but not his channel.
Mainly because he thought others would be prone to getting scammed.

He ended the video talking about some other strategies that he wanted to implement to bring more awareness to his brand.
If YouTube wasn't going to give him love, he would STILL find a way to defeat those damn guru's.

Hm...
I think the lesson is bigger than initially imagined.

The same narrative that propelled his output was the same narrative that eventually caused him to stray off track.

A narrative dependent on outside parties makes you more dependent, not independent.

Good work should make you more selfless, not selfish.
Ultimately, although this creator provided tons of value,
dependency caught up with him.

The moral I got out of all of this was to create a narrative that is
PERSONAL to you.
And keep it private.

The more private it is, there more it grows within you.
The more it grows within you, the more the narrative does the
action, not your body.
Willpower is reduced.

Now what others consider work.
You consider play.

MOVING WITHOUT FEAR

You ever played the game rock, paper, scissors?
'Yea, I have.'
You ever played *hardcode* rock, paper scissors?'
'Hm...No, I haven't.'

For the traditional game, there are 3 options:
-Rock, paper & scissors.

Rock loses to paper.
Paper loses to scissors.
Scissors loses to rock.

The hardcore version follows the same rules, with a bonus.
Rock represents a punch.
Paper represents a slap.
Scissors represent a pinch.

Lets say I am playing the game with you.
You throw out scissors.
And I throw out rock.
That means I won & I get to punch you.

That's the hardcore version of the kid's game.

I don't know if my school was the only one to adopt this or if it
was a world wide thing.
But I remember those memories as a child.

If you were a boy in my class, then you were called to play the
hardcore version of the game.
Otherwise, the other kids would make fun of you.

The skinny kids (myself included) would look terrified when we
were challenged by a big kid.
Knowing damn well, this was a game of luck.

I heard there were mental tricks to boost your chances of winning
this game.
But I didn't know any.

This was like me flipping a coin.

When I would win against a big kid, I'd punch him lightly, barely slap him or lightly pinch him.
Trying to insinuate:
'look I won't hit you hard if you don't hit me hard.'

I wished they reciprocated back....
They didn't.

My bruises stacked up.
Boys being boys.

Nowadays, I look back at that moment & laugh at it.
I think:
'yo, you were going to play the game anyways. If you're going to play, don't play scared. Play fearless.'

A med school student once gave me a trick with pain.
He said anytime you bump your toe on the wall or hurt yourself, **laugh**.
Laughing cools off the pain & you feel good.

I thought I'd give it a try the next time I was in a painful moment.

Imagine how ridiculous I looked when I once bumped my leg in the bank and started laughing like a madman.
Others looked at me like I was going to rob the place.

As ridiculous as I looked, it worked.

Laughing after hitting the wall drastically reduced my pain.
I wished I knew that as a child.

Nowadays, I try find different ways to move fearless through the bumps & bruises of life.
That's when winner qualities are cultivated.

I'm almost convinced that a level of obsession is needed in order to be great in a field.
Without it, there is a lot of wishy washy behavior.
Obsessions leads to commitment.
And commitment leads to creativity.

Obsession makes you fearless overnight.
Not fearless in every field.
But at least in 1 field.

We all have that calling with life at one point or another.
'What point is that?'

It's when you look at the mirror and ask yourself:
-Am I moving scared?
-Am I scared that I am going to get punched, slapped or pinched?
-Or am I moving in a way where I know the next rep is going to be a win?

The analogies cannot cleanly be applied from rock, paper, scissors into life.
Because with the kids game, there aren't too many tricks to refine movements.
A huge element of luck is involved.

But with learning, practicing & building your communication skills, there are tons of variables within your control.
This is what you can refine.

You're in the battlefield anyways.
Move fearless.
That's when the best reps, innovation & moves are created.

THE ART & SCIENCE OF GIVING

Giving is an art & science.
It seems like a simple process, but can easily get complicated.

'Why do you think it gets complicated?'
Because of the inability to create a distinction.

Giving & taking is a lot like creating & editing.
Let me explain.

Creating requires fearlessness & the ability to takes risks.
While editing requires humility & the ability to not takes risks.
It's night & day in terms of difference.

A person who is learning how to write for the first time
mistakenly combines the 2 into 1.
They create & edit at the same time!
Which leads to analysis paralysis.

As they are writing, a part of them is thinking:
'Geez, am I spelling correctly? Using the right grammar? Oh my!'

Not knowing that during creating, their ONLY goal is to get their
ideas out there.
And with editing, they can fix spelling, grammar, rearrange
paragraphs and all of that.

Another example I can give is with driving.
There is a clear DISTINCTION between the accelerator and the
brake..

With the accelerator, you go fast.
With the break, you go slow.

Clicking the 2 at the same time is a recipe for disaster.
And will only confuse the car.

The same process holds true with giving & taking.
The wrong mindset is to give & take at the same time.

'Why?'
Because it leads to awkward movements.

Let's say you're helping a friend move.
Physically, you are giving.
But mentally, you are thinking:
'Okay, since I'm helping this guy move, what should I ask for?'

This is the mental equivalence of clicking the accelerator & the brake at the same time.

It would be smarter to help move for the time being. Put the full focus there to the most of your abilities. Then think about taking later.

'I try to focus on the giving part, but my mind goes back to how I can take.'
That's how the mind is programmed.

THERE ARE A FEW FEATURES OF THE MIND:

Memory- ability to recall the past.

Intellect -ability to make this or that decisions.

Sensory Processor - Turn the outside world into recognizable images.

Ego - Individual Identity.

The ego is mainly focused on 'What's in it for me?'
That's not a character flaw.
That's just how the wiring is.

The process of maturity is rewiring the ego to go from:
'What's in it for me?' -> 'What's in it for us?'

It's like your palm.
Imagine what a shitshow it would be if each of the fingers were only looking out for their best interests.
Not good.

The fingers need to function together in order to form the unit of the palm.

Also, imagine if the palm is like:
'I don't need this body anymore. I want to do my own thing.'
It will be unable to.

The palm is dependent on the body for its existence.
It is in the palm's best interest to rewire the ego to think BIGGER picture.

A big part of giving is learning the art of big picture thinking.

The SECOND the palm see's that it's connected to the body, is the SECOND that it will stop thinking:
'How can I cut myself off from the body?'

Big picture thinking led to an instantaneous insight.
Giving unlocks big picture thinking.

Each time you give with the mind (to the best of your abilities) focused on giving, is each time you receive more insights into how the world works.

It's cheesy to say all the answers are 'within.'
But all the answers are within when the right intention is being exercised.
That's when infinite ideas come.
View it as **your** best interest to give.

'What about for taking?'
Taking often has a negative connotation assigned to it.
But it shouldn't.

The more the palm does what it's supposed to do.
In this case, the palm is used to hold the spoon which will feed the body....

The more nutrients the palm will get.
Nothing negative about the matter.

Taking is seen in a positive light when giving was done with the right intention.

A person who is waiting on their oil change with an awful attitude is not being patient, they are just waiting.
Waiting is physical.
Patience is mental.

Check yourself when you are physically giving, but mentally...you are plotting how you will take.

You'll know because the body will feel more restricted.
And the moves will be harder to execute.

At that moment, remind yourself that when you give, give.
When you take, take.
It's 2 different hats for a reason.

Learning the essence of giving & taking is what makes a charismatic superstar.
A person who creates opportunities for themselves & others.

OUT OF SIGHT, OUT OF MIND

There are different ways to deal with betrayal.

Some choose revenge.

Others choose to ignore.

I understand the philosophy of revenge.

It makes intellectual & emotional sense to me.

However, I often talk about the art of ignoring.

One of the most popular blogs I wrote is called **'Ignoring Someone Who Hurt you.'**

'Why do you choose ignoring over revenge?'

Because revenge requires creativity.

And the more I entertain revenge, the more I use my number 1 asset (my mind) to think about someone I despise.

The beauty about Out of Sight, Out of Mind is that it works with another life cliché:

'Which is?'

Time heals all.

With time, the senses start to forget or reduce the distaste of the betrayal.

This allows for the moving on process to exponentially rise.

Also, Out of Sight Out of Mind is a beautiful concept to cross apply to the world of following up.

This daily email list initially started off with doubt.

I had a roommate in 2019 who said:

'You have to write daily emails because everyone else is doing it.'

Not sure how long you have been on this list... but I used to write weekly emails.

I told him daily was too much.

He said something like:

'Just try it out man. Trust me. You'll always be on the mind of your top readers.'

At first, I was hesitant.

No way could I write every day.

However, he was right.

The daily emails play a crucial role in this business.

A lot of the short stories get passed onto my books as well.

Nowadays, marketers are talking about this concept called 'Media Stacking.'

As if it's something new.

To be fair, that phrase is new to me.

I had no clue what it was.

But I was doing it when I was cross combining these newsletters with my books & promoting it on YouTube videos, blogs and podcasts.

This is when media becomes connected.

Did you know that the average person consumes 5-7 hours of media a day??

That's ranging from tv shows, radio, podcasts, newspapers etc.

I don't think you understand what a **colossal** number that really is!

Here's a lesson for social skills.

Be a part of that media to stay in their minds.

This is not to say you start a YouTube channel and write books.

Instead, be the first to message.

Aka: Following up.

Following up is pretty much staying in their media realm.

Because here's one cliché I don't fully agree with:

'You are the average of your 5 best friends.'

I don't find that to be fully accurate.

When you listen to that quote too much, you start evaluating your friends from your desires too much.

If your desire it to become a top tier entrepreneur...

A part of you may judge your close friends for having 9-5 jobs.

Then you'll repeat:

'Oh no, I'm the average of these 5 people. I'll never be a top tier entrepreneur with these bums by my side!

This will cause you to undermine the value that they do bring.

'What quote do you like more?'
I like the quote:
You are the average of the content that you consume.

Not saying that friends do not play a role on someone's psyche.

Negative people do play a poor role.

But I think what isn't talked about enough is the role that media plays.

After the day is up, the friends leave.

After the day is up, the phone stays.

When I realized a person is what type of media they consume (and put faith in) I saw why following up is more crucial in today's landscape.

People get busy.

Their attention is being pulled in all directions.

It's rarely personal when they didn't respond back.

Follow up bud, they may respond back then.

USING SHOCK TO LEARN STORYTELLING

In my book, **The Art and Science of Storytelling,** I made a shocking confession.

The shocking confession was:

For a storyteller, no content is bad content.

'Even the shocking ones?'

Even the shocking ones.

There were 2 types of content which I found very shocking:

1. How to Catch a Predator.

2. Britney Spears in 2007.

Around the 2007 era, content was centralized.

When I went to school, I'd know what everyone was watching.

One show everyone was talking about was, How to Catch a Predator.

It was a show hosted by Chris Hansen.

Chris and his team would set up local stings in neighborhoods to catch adults who were trying to solicit sex from minors.

The team would chat with these adults under a fake identity and convince the adults to meet them at this house.

Once the adults came to the house, the cameras were **on.**

Once they entered, rather than hanging with the minor, they would be having a conversation with Chris Hansen.

There were a few shocking things about the show:

1. You were seeing someone's life getting ruined in real time.

2. The predators often looked like Average Joe's. Doctors, engineers & plumbers.

3. Since the show was on MSNBC, the entire U.S would be seeing it.

As Chris Hansen interrogated the predators to see why they did it, they'd often say:

-I wanted to mentor her.

-I seriously wasn't going to do anything.

-I thought she was of age.

So, you even got a chance to see people lying.

This show made you see the dark parts of reality.

Another pretty shocking moment was with Britney Spears in 2007ish.

Back then, Britney was seen as the symbol of a top tier superstar.

She had a string of hits, was multitalented & easy on the eyes.

All should be peachy with her in terms of media coverage, right?

Nope!

The media turned on her & she was having a mental breakdown for the world to see.

I'm not sure if the negative media coverage led to the mental breakdown or the mental breakdown led to the negative media coverage.

One of the images I clearly remember was when she shaved her head and was hitting a car with an umbrella.

To Catch a Predator & the Britney Spears events led me to understanding how you can use all emotions to color a plot.

Using emotions and cross combining it with characters leads to emergence.

Emergence is when 2 different components are combined to create something entirely new.

An example is chocolate milk.

I used to have this cocoa powder that I would put in my milk.

Once I put the powder in the milk, there was no going back.

In terms of shocking content, you get to see, feel & experience dark emotions of others.

Be empathetic when need be.

However, also know that dark emotions are just as useful for a storyteller as the light emotions.

That dark emotions can be combined with other characters to create a NEW plot.

The plot is an act of creativity & difficult (if not impossible) to trace back to the source.

Overall, shocking content is not always pretty to others.

However, for the storyteller, it's just another data point that will level up our game & help us create more compelling content.

EXPLAINING THINGS ELEGANTLY

You ever had that moment when you needed someone to explain something to you.

And all they did was confuse you?

They gave fragmented pieces of data.

0 examples.

0 analogies.

After they were done, they looked back at you with this goofy smirk like they did a great job.

They did a good job showing how smart they are.

But as a teacher, they **failed**.

There are 3 steps to explaining things clearly:

1. Know the topic.

2. Meet the student where they are.

3. Strategic engagement.

1 is common sense. You can't explain something you don't know.

2 requires controlling your ego. This is when you meet the student where they are so it's easier to use simple language and breathtaking analogies.

3 is when you ask questions like, 'am I making sense?'

I would like to add a phantom step before even thinking about executing these 3.

'What's that?'
Make sure the person **wants** to learn.

Fire does not light up wet wood.
Fire lights up dry wood.

Wet wood is a mind that is not curious.
Fire is a mind that is curious.

You trying to force someone to be interested is a losing game.
They will not ask the right questions or show enthusiasm.
At best, you can explain to these people for practice.

'I need to practice? I thought it would be easy to explain things if I knew the topic well?'
Nope!

You need to practice.
And you need to practice a lot.

Explaining things is equivalent to painting a canvas in someone's mind.
You think a painter just got like that willy nilly?

Nah, they had to practice.

This is the era where I think more people are going to get curious about some form of content creation.
Whether it's tweeting, writing a book, recording a YouTube video etc.

Most importantly, explaining things is fun.

I can't stress that enough.

When you are explaining a topic, it's like you are untangling a rope in your mind & making YOURSELF smarter.

Yes....

You're explain things for yourself too, not only for others.

If you are nervous to speak up at work, nervous to handle your first consulting client or nervous to publish your first YouTube video, then:

-Focus less on yourself.

-And focus more on the content.

Rather than asking:

'How can I get others to like what I have to say?'

Ask:

'How can I explain this topic CRYSTAL CLEAR?'

Never Reward Laziness

Last year, there was a day I went to Target.
And it had already been a long day.

What started off as a routine day ended up becoming a pain in
the ass.

My camera randomly stopped working.
So I bought a new one.

And when I bought a new one, it required a new SD card.
Those cards that allow your camera to transfer its files to the
laptop.

Getting the new camera took longer than expected.
The people in Best Buy knew their products as well as I did...

Not well.

**So by the time I was at Target, there was agitation being
built.**

Good news was that I found the SD card quickly and bought it
even faster.

This was one of those Targets on the second floor.
Where you need to park in a garage... then walk upstairs.
'Why is that important info?'
For the next thing I'm about to say....

As I am walking downstairs after my purchase, I see 2 little kids.
They seem to be brothers.

I see the younger one of the 2 lifting his bicycle up the stairs.
He put the bike around his shoulder and is gliding up the stairs
with grace.

Then there is the other kid...
Just sitting their twiddling his thumbs.

As I am walking downstairs, he is like:
'Hey man, you mind taking this upstairs for me?'

I look at the guy.
Seems to be a healthy guy.

I ask him why he doesn't take it upstairs like the other kid?

And in pure honesty, he's like:
'Because I don't feel like it.'

I laugh and say no.
And go about my day...

'You said no? Come on man, that was messed up! He was just a little kid.'
Exactly.

At that age, that's when peak energy should be unleashed.
A kid should be gliding up the stairs with that bike.
Just like the younger one.

This kid wanted a handout.
He wanted me to rescue him from this situation.

Imagine if that was the case.
That I did lift that bike and take it upstairs.

What next?
What about when he has to go downstairs?

He will once again sit their idle, twiddling his thumbs...
Passively waiting until someone comes to rescue him.

Never reward lazy behavior.
And ironically, that's the kindest thing to do.

Rewarding lazy behavior has a word.
And it's called "enabling."

Enabling is dangerous because it's a silent killer.
One of those odorless poisons....

You can't tell when it's near you.
Yet, it's killing you slowly.

I have no clue what that kid did after I left.
I wonder if there was a bit of a dog in him...
I wonder if he saw the other kid (who was much smaller) putting in the work..
And if that made him get into action?

I can't tell.

This is why bootstrapping is a real world school in my book.
When you put your own money up & your own hours into a personal project.

That's when there is an investment.

-Without personal investment, it's too easy to ask for handouts.
-With personal investment, it becomes personal.

A winner knows how to make it personal with the man or woman in the mirror.

A loser makes it personal with others that they are cool with or with people they have never met.

Constant competition mindset.
Burning bridges and further fueling the ego.

When going on a competition with the self, that's when an inner dog is unleashed.
And fire, consistency, creativity are the rewards.

A person will never declare a sacred war against themselves when they are lazy.
Or when they were enabled.

Coddling causes 2 people to lose:
-The one being coddled.
-The one doing the coddling.

The one doing the coddling is the more sinister one in this case
because they have more knowledge than the person being
coddled.

Tough love creates wimps.
Tough love creates winners.

At the end of the day, tough love has stood the test of time,
because it will always bring out the best in those who wanted to
shine all along.

IS WATCHING FILM A HOBBY?

For actors, screenwriters and film producers, watching film is a
high ROI act.

That's because movies serve as creative insights and a new way of
doing things.

These creative professions build their film grammar and learn
along the way.
But is this the case for the average person?

The average person is someone with no acting, screenwriting or
film producing desires.

*I believe it can still be high ROI as long as the person knows
what to look out for.*

These creative professionals are not only watching film to gain
access to low level details...

Plenty of them are just watching with their body.

I had a high school gym teacher who would always drill a concept
into his basketball players minds...

This gym teacher taught gym in the day.
And at night, he would coach the basketball team.

I felt like my school didn't want to get a real coach.
So they got this guy.
Coach Ray.

I don't know why I didn't view him as a real coach.
He technically was.

He used to play college basketball before his career ending injury.
Went thru depression after his injury.

Coach Ray was struggling to find a line of work until he became
my gym teacher.

When he found out the basketball team needed a coach, he enthusiastically agreed.
And bought his knowledge of the game with him.

Coach Ray was known for having the team watch film.
Sometimes, they would watch film more than practice!

He wasn't a low level detail guy though.
Coach taught people to watch the film with the body.

Go with the feel.
Go with the 'gestalt' of things.

This must have worked because the players showed rapid signs of improvement under Coach Ray's methods.

His strategy is like a lot of these actors and such.
Watch with the body.

Watch with the body does not mean let your mind drift off in lala land.

It means to spot those moments which **light** up the body.
Those are the things to look out for.

This lighting up of the body are the feelings that generate in different areas.
On those moments in the film, that's when you zone in.

What did the director do?
How did the scene change?
And did the plot develop in any way?

This allows the consumer to enjoy the film **and** learn.
Rather than just taking notes the entire time & ruining the experience.

Being a participant in any sort of platform requires creativity.
No way around that.
Blogging, youtubing, podcasting, tweeting etc.

Creativity comes from many places.

Within and outside.

Within is during introspection, reflection, meditation.
Outside is thru learning, watching and doing.

All faculties raised up leads to a peak creative all-star.
One that can learn quickly.

10 years ago, telling someone to watch film to be more productive
would have sounded asinine.

"Don't do that! Learn to code or learn Microsoft excel. Those are
productive tasks."

They are productive tasks.
No denying that.

But the spectrum of productive tasks has dramatically increased
in the information age.

And nothing was the same....

In the internet age, creativity is the hottest commodity.
And the body serves a crucial role in mining that commodity to
the max.

CAN ENEMIES BECOME FRIENDS?

I had this one cousin in New York who used to crack me up.
Something about him was very intense.

He lived in Queens.
And in a pretty tough neighborhood.

Whenever my family would visit him, he would show me around.
He would take me to the basketball courts to play.

This was a stage when he was very religious.
He wore a punjabi, grew out his beard a ton, and wore sandals.

I would ask him if he would change before we went to play
basketball.
And he looked at me like I was crazy.
He'd be like *'I AM wearing my basketball clothes.'*

You're going to wear that??
You look like you are about to convert someone to a new religion.
Not play basketball.

We headed to the courts.

In the courts, I could see a bunch of the players laughing at us.
This particular cousin looked very old.
I was 16 at the time.
And he looked like he could be my dad.

A lot of kids would challenge us to a 2 on 2 game.
They thought we would be light work.

I was a bit embarrassed to be seen around my cousin.
He looked ridiculous on the court dressed like that.

But I wasn't embarrassed when he started playing.

My cousin was a great basketball player.
Aggressive, fast and excellent decision maker.

It was comical seeing myself, and a guy who looked like my dad's brother in law, schooling players who actually looked like they belonged on the court.
These were the streets of Jamaica, Queens!

Great memories.

After our games, my cousin would take me to a sandwich spot.
The he would tell me a list of his enemies.

'Enemies? What the hell, why?'
I have no clue why.

But my cousin had a lot of enemies.
People that didn't like him.

Old friend's who turned their back on him.
Exes.
And kids who he never knew throwing dirt on his name.

Why?
I have no clue.

I think it had to do with my cousin's intense personality.
Unless you knew him, you would maybe despise him too.
From body language, to the content of his message...
Just a very, "in your face" kind of guy.

My cousin's philosophy was that enemies should never be forgiven.
They must be destroyed.
And if not destroyed, never forgiven.
The mere thought of forgiveness was a sin in his world.

He also wanted his family to view his enemies as their enemies.
There were times he wanted me to help him beat someone up.

I politely declined.

My cousin's philosophy works for him.
But for me, I don't dwell over people who dislike me too much.

I guard my mind.

I have a themed mind.

'What is a themed mind?'
What is the theme of this email?
'About enemies.'
Can you hold a theme?
'No.'
Can you touch it?
'No.'

But it is an underlying thread of unity.
This thread of unity allows me to seamlessly plug in the sentences.

Without the theme, I'd be having a bunch of sentences which did not plug in.

A themed mind is a mind that has a purpose.
A grander vision.
And all thoughts are sentences which plug into that vision.
That's what I gear my mind towards.

The sky is blue but sometimes I wonder if it's pink.
^ This line makes no sense to this email.
It's an unnecessary line.

And I am able to spot the unnecessary line very quickly because a theme is there.

But for a mind without a theme?
That ridiculous line will be entertained.
Or worse, it will be confused as a main component of the story.

I've had plenty of enemies in my life.
Some, my doing.
Others were formed because I did nothing.

In the social world, nothing is something.

Let's say someone wants a free consult call & you ignore their message.
The ignoring did not go unnoticed.

Plenty of snakes are born that way.

And other ways enemies were formed was thru 'he said, she said.'
Let's say a bitter ex or former friend spills lies about you.

Everyone has enemies.
Whether we are aware or not.
Even the most saintly soul.

My philosophy on enemies is subtle unlike my cousin.
I let them do them.
And I do me.
Rather than attacking them.

And I'm not a big fan of allowing them to enter my life even if we
reach a peace treaty.
For what?

Some people have an abundance mindset on people.
Some have a scarcity mindset on people.

People with scarcity mindset will not only forgive their enemy.
But go grab drinks and all that with them.

I'm not using the term 'scarcity' in a rude manner.
But that's just not me.

My philosophy has always been a smaller friend circle over a
bigger one.
And a bigger acquaintance circle over a smaller one.

A former enemy is like a dynamite.
Sometimes, the dynamite will not go off.
And sometimes, it will.

I had this guy on Twitter a few years ago talking shit about me
because I used the phrase 'emotional intelligence' in a few of my
tweets.

He kept tagging me and talking about how dumb I was.
I never blocked him.
Just let him talk into the winds.

Later on, he started tagging me in articles about 'emotional intelligence' and saying that he thought I would find it interesting.
Trying to get all buddy buddy.

Social skills is not always about making friends.
It's also about learning when not to make friends.

Haters are moody.
Enemies are moodier.

My cousin and I have different perceptions of enemies.
He has an active approach.
I have a more laid back passive approach.

An enemy will probably present themselves to you at one point or another.
Or they probably have.

There's no right or wrong answers to social skills.
It comes down to knowing your style & what works best for the theme of your mind.

THE STORYTELLER'S WEAPON

Having a theme is the weapon for a storyteller.

With the theme, the content just falls out.

Without the theme, the content creation process feels impossible.

What is the theme?

It's a general message.

What's the gist of what you are trying to say?

You can always get more specific from there.

One great example of themes is from the recent Fresh Prince of Bel Air remake.

When the announcement of the remake was made, there were mixed reviews.

A lot of it was negative.

People were like:

'This doesn't seem like a comedy to me!'

Well, that's the point.

The new Fresh Prince of Bel Air has a **different theme.**

I saw an episode recently on the Peacock app and was surprised with the twist.

I liked it a lot.

It had a gritty & dark *gist*.

Even though a lot of the characters are the same...

The theme being drastically different leads to a **completely new** experience for the consumer.

So, if you are struggling with writing or speaking for a speech or a book coming up.

Don't go more specific.

Go general.

What is the GIST of what you are trying to say?

That's reverse engineering in the content creation world.

LETTING BYGONES BE BYGONES

When I was a little kid, I would go to a thing called dawat's.

Dawat's are when uncle's and auntie's host a party and invite their friends.

The kids gather in one room and find a way to entertain themselves.

One way to entertain ourselves was to fight and record it.

At the time, professional wrestling was at a fever pitch.

Any kid who was a somebody wanted to be a wrestler.

There was one guy who would bring his big ugly camcorder to the dawat.

Then the kids would choose the fights that made sense.

My brother and I would get paired up to wrestle the other brothers.

The dawat's would have 15 to 20 kids.

So, we'd have an audience too.

One day, my brother and I got paired up to fight with another pair of brothers who were roughly our size.

It was a tossup as to who was going to win.

My brother pulled me to the side and said:

'We have speed on our side. Let's use that to our advantage.'

Once the fight began, we circled the other 2 and began to run away from them.

This got them winded.
Once they got winded, we **pounced**.

My brother punched the other big brother.
I snuck behind the other little brother and choked him till he submitted.
Once he submitted, me and my brother were declared the winner.

After that, the other kids were impressed.
Once of them said:
'These are the wrestle mania brothers.'

From there on out, when we would go to dawat's, we were known as the wrestle mania brothers.

Since I was such a dork in school then...
Having this title gave me some pride.

One day, I go to a civil dawat.
The kids weren't fighting away.
We were dressed up in formal clothes.

That's when a kid named Asif made fun of the way that I tied my tie.
The others looked at him like:
'Huh....don't you know?? That's one of the wrestle mania brothers!!'

I let the title get to my head and was like:
'If you have a problem with my tie, then we can settle it in the ring.'

Asif gladly accepted.

Fighting Asif was considered foolish on my end.

He was way bigger than me.

However, his insult got under my skin and I wasn't going to let him off so easily.

The other kids got excited.

Finally, a wrestling match in this boring ass dawat.

A kid named Jim volunteered to be the announcer.

I rolled up my sleeves

Put my tie in my pocket.

Stretched a little.

Asif did the same.

The kids surrounded us.

Jim began his introductions.

He was like:

'On one side of the corner, we have the man, the myth, the legend.. Asif!!'

The crowd went wild.

Then he says:

'On the other side, we have the pussy.... Arman!'

The crowd busted out laughing.

When he called me a pussy, I completely forgot about Asif's disrespect towards me and punched Jim right on the nose.

It was instinct.

Jim began bleeding from his nose.
The audience members gasped.

Jim looked shocked.
Then his shocked face turned into him crying very loudly.

He went downstairs yelling:
'Ammu, ammu!'
Which meant mom, mom.

My heart started beating fast.
If he was going to be crying like that, then he was definitely going to snitch on me.
My mom would find out.

That's when I hear my mom's voice:
'Arman! Come downstairs right now.'

I didn't want to go downstairs.
But the other kids consoled me and told me that there was no hiding.
So, I went downstairs to receive my punishment.

That memory was from over 15 years ago.
Asif and I still talk to this day.
Jim and I still talk to this day.

Whenever I got to West Palm, I play basketball with my childhood friends.

Jim always rolls by.

Once we are done with the games, we stand by the parking lot and talk.

We share a lot of memories of the old school days.

Routinely, Jim and I recall the memory of me punching him on the nose.

Sometimes, I tell the story.

Sometimes, he tells the story.

He tells it way better than me.

We have let bygones be bygones.

Which means:

-To forgive past conflicts.

I can't empathize with someone who says:

'I have nothing to say.'

Of course, you do.

I'm sure you could relate to this story.

Maybe you're like:

'Whoa, I used to have wrestling matches with my friends too!'

But a lot of people stop there.

They get the content then begin twiddling their thumbs like:

'Uh...Now what?'

Now what is that you find the **context** behind the content.
What is the lesson that you learned?

From the story with Asif and Jim, I learned a bunch of lessons:

- Titles can fuel pride.
- Anger can make you do something rash.
- Dark moments can turn into funny moments.
- Funny moments can be shared as stories in the present or the future.
- It's never too late to let bygones be bygones.

By spotting the content AND the context, you will understand the essence of storytelling.

IMPORTANCE OF FINDING A HOBBY

Recently, my AC broke.
The lowest it would go to was 79 degrees.

I went along with this for a few weeks.
Was too busy to call an AC repairman.
Wanted to see what I could do to fix it myself.

I didn't really try to fix it much myself.
I just changed the batteries on the thermostat and that was about it.

My strategy didn't fix the AC.

Yesterday, I had enough!
I decided to call the go-to handyman for my area.
Bill was his name.

Bill texted back and made it seem like my AC breaking was an urgent matter.
'I will be there IMMEDIATELY,' he wrote.

And he was true to his word.
Soon, he was knocking on my door.
He was an elderly man.
More on that shortly.

For the next 35 minutes, he was toggling with a bunch of wires and replacing some stuff.

He said to me:

'This is more serious than I thought. I need to get the AC man involved.'

I asked him if he knew an AC man.

He looked at me like I was an idiot.

'Yes, I know the AC man. He's my brother. Just called him. He will be here immediately.'

And once again, Bill was true to his word.

The AC man came asap.

This new guy looked roughly around Bill's age.

He looked at the same vicinity Bill was looking at then said:

'I need to go to the roof.'

Then he went to the roof.

Soon, he texted Bill and Bill said to me:

'Problem solved.

Suddenly, I felt cool air permeating my living facility.

As Bill was cleaning up, I asked him how he learned to fix an AC.

He scoffed at the question.

*'I know how to fix more than that. If **anything** breaks in your living area, call me. I will fix it.'*

I was expecting him to charge me a lot of money.

When I asked him how much, he said:

'Oh, it's free.'

Free?
I thought something like this would require payment.

But no.
Bill was retired.
He did this for fun.

As he was wrapping up, he said:
'I am 87 years old. If I didn't do this, then I'd be bored.'

Fixing was Bill's hobby.
And Bill's hobby was what kept him young.

He looked like he was in his 80s.
But his spirit was that of someone in their mid-20s.

Too much free time is not a good thing.
It makes someone age faster and become more annoying.

In an alternate reality...
If Bill just took his pension checks and stayed home to watch tv
all day, I'm pretty sure he would have aged much faster.

Remember the 2nd law of thermodynamics.
'A closed system gravitates towards entropy (disorder). New
knowledge and energy should constantly be added into a closed
system to fight entropy and grow towards profitability.'

'English please Armani!'

Your room for example.

If you don't do anything to your room for 1 month...

I guarantee it will naturally become messier, not cleaner.

Any system is like that.

You need to actively clean your room to fight the entropy (messiness).

If Bill just stayed home all day and did nothing, his mind would have been prone to disorder.

But by investing in the hobby of fixing things, he needs to constantly be learning new things.

When I asked him how he learned to fix stuff, he initially said he went to school for it.

But then he said:

'But I'm self-taught now. Things I learned in school are outdated. I need to stay updated with the newest strategies.'

Therefore, Bill is bringing in knowledge and energy into his internal world, which allows him to offset the disorder and remain forever young.

When you are feeling stressed and annoyed, then chances are that you don't have too much on you plate.

But rather, because you have too little on your plate...

BECOMING A SUPERSTAR IN YOUR ROLE

I played a few sports growing up.
The one I gravitated towards the most was basketball.

The thing I loved about basketball was that you never knew what someone was capable of.
It's a sport where you should **not** judge a book by its cover.

I went hooping at a placed called Lake Lytal.
There were all walks of life that would come and hoop.

Some of these guys looked like they shouldn't be hooping.
One guy was this heavy old man with a big belly.

He wasn't old really.
But by basketball standards... he was old.
Roughly 40 ish.

He'd want to play with the 20 years olds.
We'd look at him and think:
'He doesn't seem like he can go up and down a full court game.'

We were right.

He couldn't run up and down in a full court game.
But he didn't need to.

This 40-year-old man was VERY precise with his moves.
He'd make efficient dribbles and sharp passes.

A lot of people in Lake Lytal had the ego mentality.
Whenever they had the ball, they wanted to shoot.

But this 40-year-old man was looking to pass first.

Seeing him pass with such grace instilled a different mindset on the team he was playing for.
Soon, whenever he was volunteering for a pickup game, he was one of the first picks.

-He wasn't the fastest.
-He wasn't the best shooter.
-He couldn't do lockdown defense on you.

But he could pass and instill a teamwork mentality.
He knew his role and overperformed his role.

The tough part is spotting your role.
Many times, someone probably told you what you do best.
But the ego shut it down.

'I pass well, so what? Basketball is all about shooting!'

The ego plays tricks like that.
But take some time and spot the role.
That's #1.

Then becoming a **superstar** in the role is #2.

The guy didn't just pass and call it a day.

He had passes that changed the morale of the ENTIRE game.

Therefore, see how your individualized role impacts the entire system!

By grounding yourself in your own greatness, it becomes much easier to expand.

Now when you are expanding, you lead with your strengths first...rather than your weaknesses.

THE FEELING OF ACCOMPLISHMENT

-Gratitude is built from true knowledge.

-When you really know something, you're amazed that anything works at all.

May 2017, I was going to be moving to a new place.

My brother and I kept hearing about this place called IKEA.

But we never went in.

We heard that they sold furniture for cheap.

Might as well check it out.

Once we went inside IKEA, we were amazed.

It was a great atmosphere.

They had unique displays that bought the furniture to life.

The products were very affordable.

I set a certain budget and was going to have a lot of money remaining after we made the purchases for our place.

Once we were at the checkout, the IKEA man was like:

'Would you like to pay X amount more money in order for us to assemble it for you?'

I thought the items would be very easy to set up.

So, I said:

'Nah, don't worry about it.'

A few days pass and the IKEA people come by and begin dropping items off to the new place.

We get the boxes.

I was amazed.

Not in a good way though....

The items were way more complicated to set up than I thought.

From the sofa, to the TV stand, to my queen-sized bed.

Ah... the queen-sized bed.

It looked so amazing on the display.

Now I was going to be spending my whole day setting it up?

I dragged the big brown box upstairs.

Then I dragged the big mattress upstairs.

Bought some screws and such.

Took out the user manual with the tiny font.

It was time to assemble.

I was pissed.

If I knew it was going to be this complicated, then I would have just told the guy that I'd pay extra to have it assembled.

But now I was on my own.

This ended up taking the entire Saturday.

There were a few times when I was almost done with the assembling to realize that I did step 5 wrong.

Since I did step 5 wrong, step 27 was compromised.

Damn...

That's when I began undoing my hard work and redoing the steps.

But this time, when I re-entered step 5, I was a smarter version of myself.

Step 6,7,8 and so on didn't take as long.

It's because I **knew** how to do it.

Step by step, I slowly saw the mattress coming to life.

As I was getting closer to the finish line, I felt happy for not having the IKEA team assemble it.

I'm happy that I assembled it myself.

Nowadays, when I lie on the bed, I like knowing that I took part in shaping it.

This was a great feeling.

The feeling of accomplishment.

WHAT ALL STORYTELLERS KNOW

I recall a few years back, I discovered one of the funniest inside jokes. It's called:

'I don't care what anyone says about you, but you're good in my book.'

One time, I went out with a few fraternity brothers in Miami.

The cool thing about being in a fraternity is that you always have a tribe no matter where you go.

I let them know I'm in town.

They pick me up and take me out to eat.

Then we go out afterwards.

We are walking around, and I make a joke.

I go up to a guy named Saj and am like:

'I don't care what anyone says about you, but you're good in my book.'

No clue why I did that.

But afterwards, he was like:

'What? What do people say about me?'

I didn't say anything.

Eventually, he got jittery.

He went to others and was like:

'Yo, has anyone been saying anything about me? Be honest.'

I completely made it up as a joke.

But it really bothered him.

Then I was like:

'Bro, no one said anything about you. I was just poking fun.'

A few months go by, and this time, the Miami brothers came to Tampa.

Saj still remembered the inside joke.

He went to one of the Tampa guys and was like:

'Look Matt, I don't' care what anyone says about you, but you're good in my book.'

Then Matt was like:

'What? What do people say about me?'

Seeing the identical reaction was hilarious!!

From Saj's perspective, I knew something that he didn't know.

And due to that tension, automatically, his narrative mind was engaged.

That's why gossiping is a thing.

One party knows more information than the other party.

Your storytelling skills magnify your character.

You can use knowing a lot for sinister motives or for pure motives.

The main thing is that:

The storyteller always knows more than the audience.

TOO SMART FOR YOUR OWN GOOD

When I was in the 10th grade, I had a friend named Omar.
He was a strange fellow.

He was a black kid from Canada who was **very quiet** mixed with **very hilarious.**

There were 3 kids in my classes who would get in trouble a lot.
It was Jared, Kyle and Omar.

With Jared and Kyle, you could expect it.
Those 2 were normally outspoken and loved attention.

But Omar in a conversation was SOOOO quiet.
He was a mute when you had him in a 1 on 1 setting.

So it was strange seeing him become a class clown.
He'd brazenly tell jokes and misbehave in front of the teachers.

It's as though he had a split personality.

One day, I am chilling in a class where we got done early for the day.
I go to a computer and begin surfing the web.
Next to me, Omar is sitting with a CD player listening to music.

I asked Omar what he was listening to.

He quickly said:
'Myself.'

I thought this was his way of avoiding a convo.
I go back to the computer.

He looks at me a bit disappointed that I didn't follow up.
He began bopping his head like he was really enjoying this song.

After seeing him enjoy the music like that, I asked him again:
'What are you listening to?'

He once again said, *'myself.'*

I was like:
'Yea right! Are you a musician?'

He said:
'Yea...'

I asked him if I could listen.
He seemed like he was waiting for me to ask him that.
He puts his headset around my ears.

Then I hear the song....

The song was of a guy rapping about Martin Luther King.
The lyrics were deep.
It had a great instrumental.

The more I heard the song, the more I felt like it could be Omar, but wasn't sure.

Was this guy really a rapper?

I said:

'This song is fire, but that's definitely not you!!'

He said:

'Yea, it is.'

I asked what his rap name was.

He said:

'Nameless.'

Yea okay....

That's definitely not him.

He told me he had a Myspace music page.

I said he probably got another rapper's songs that he put on his page.

He was **aggressively** trying to convince me that he was a rapper.

I mean, was it is so outlandish to think he was telling the truth?

Thus far, Omar had been an enigma.

A mute who turns into a class clown when people are around.

What if he was actually a rapper?

I told him I'd believe him if he said my name in one of his songs.

I didn't care if he roasted me or whatever.

But I had to hear my name, otherwise, he wasn't Nameless.

He said:

'Okay.'

I went home and told my brother about the incident.

It just so happened that my brother knew Omar's brother.

Omar was in my class.

And Darren was in my brother's class.

My brother told me that Omar being a rapper was not as weird as it sounded…

Because Darren was a rapper.

He was???

Now I was really mind blown.

Back then, this was big news.

There wasn't Soundcloud, Spotify and all of that.

If you had a CD with songs, then you were considered talented.

Especially if you had the skill to back it up.

A week passes by.

Omar taps me on the shoulder.

He gives me a CD.

I go home with the CD.

I needed a CD player to play it.

My brother and I listen to the song together.

It was the same voice I heard in class that day.
The guy was insulting someone.

I heard a lot of lyrics.
But I didn't hear my name....

Until...
The end of the song.

The rapper said:
'What's good Arman?'

Then he starts rhyming my name with a bunch of words that rhyme with Arman.
It was a machine gun of roasts.
Then the song ends.

I was amazed!
Couldn't believe.
I soon became a huge Nameless fan and began telling the other kids in the class about his skills.

One day, I'm playing basketball at a park right by my school.
Omar and Darren come through.

Omar introduced me to his brother.
I meet Darren who seems like a more sociable version of Omar.

Once we are done playing, Darren told me he was supposed to meet Kanye West next week.

I didn't know if he was lying or telling the truth.

But being a naïve teenager, I asked:

'When you meet him, can you get me his autograph? I am a big fan of his music.'

I cringe thinking about asking that question.

If Darren's meeting Kanye, I'm pretty sure it's to advance his own career... not to get an autograph for someone he just met.

That's when Darren says:

'Ha, I think Kanye is overrated. He needs to....'

Darren began using these overly technical phrases.

He began convincing me why I shouldn't like Kanye's music.

One unheard of adjective followed by one unheard of noun.

All I head was jibber jabber.

I was like:

This guy is too smart for his own good.

Here's the thing.

Darren was smart.

He was musically gifted.

But to me...he's someone who's too smart for his own good.

When you're too smart for your own good, you find it difficult to empathize with a beginner.

A few years ago, Martin Scorsese said that Avengers was *technically* not a film.

This was when Avengers was on FIRE.

It was setting unprecedented records.

When Scorsese made that comment, he was crucified.

But Scorsese stood by his comments.

I thought it was ridiculous to say that.

But after learning more about film, Scorsese
was *technically* right.

Film is something that normally appeals to a narrow group of
people because it was created with the intention of being art.

While the opposite of a film is something that is created with the
intention of capturing a broad audience.

Did Scorsese have the technicalities right?

Yes.

But was he also someone who was too smart for his own good?

In my opinion, *yes.*

'What determines if someone is too smart for their own good?'

**It's when their advanced knowledge is being force fed
upon a beginner.**

The beginner doesn't know the crevices of the craft.

They just assess:

- Do I like it or not?

Maybe if I knew all the details about rap like Darren did, I'd be
like:

'Yes, Kanye is overrated.'

But I didn't know the rap technicalities at that time.

Darren was unable to see that.

He only saw from his lens.

Being too smart is **not** a good thing.

Because the same knowledge that fueled you is the same knowledge that can blind you...

WORK FOR KNOWLEDGE, NOT GLAMOUR

I had this coworker named Neil in one of my past jobs.

He was this larger than life personality who knew how to tell stories.

He would call me *bud* a lot.

'Hey bud, you still with me?'

He'd ask me that question when he'd tell a story.

He'd ask me that question when he was teaching me on the job.

Since most of my team was in Chicago, he was in charge of getting me caught up to speed.

I would often have calls with him in the video conference room.

He had very serious eye contact.

One day, he was like:

'Armani, would you like a stretch project?'

Eager me was like:

'Hell yea I want a stretch project!! But what's a stretch project?'

Then he told me that these are projects that new employees should do to make a name for themselves.

They were not mandatory.

However, a newbie doing stretch projects will bring visibility.

I was like:

'Sure! Since I'm over here in Tampa, it's hard to make my name known.'

So, Neil gave me a bunch of tasks to do.

And I eagerly did them.

3 weeks goes on by.

Neil logs out for the day.

Now there is a guy named Joseph training me.

I told Joseph that I was working on a stretch project.

Once I told him what the stretch project included, Joseph became **furious**.

Joseph was Neil's senior.

After he heard my announcement, he was like:

'Armani, you aren't doing a stretch project. You are just doing Neil's grunt work!!'

When I heard that, I was sad.

I thought the work I was doing had impact.

Then the sadness turned into anger.

Here I am working extra hard to do another man's grunt work?

What BS!!

Younger me was upset.

But nowadays, I'm like:

'Who cares if you were doing someone else's grunt work? What exactly do you think an apprenticeship is?'

Read these books and watch these documentaries.

When a newbie finds a master to work with, do you think the master has the newbie doing glamour work from the beginning?

Absolutely not.

They make the newbie do the grunt work to get a FEEL for how things work.

That's just how it is.

After doing the grunt work for Neil, ironically, I was getting smarter.

I was no longer the new guy at work who was quiet on the calls.

I was speaking up because I was answering the questions that the others couldn't.

Reports that the other veterans didn't touch in *years* were the reports I just got done finalizing a few *hours* ago.

This was an **opportunity**.

But younger me didn't see it.

All I saw was someone taking advantage of me.

Maybe Neil was looking out for me, I'm not sure.

But what I do know is that I accidentally ended up doing what Neil said!

He said stretch projects would make my name **known**.

And by doing the work no one else wanted to do, I began to make my name **known**.

Bottom line:

- All fields have grunt work.

Just like the famous saying goes:
One person's trash is another man's treasure.

My remix is:
One person's grunt work is another person experience.

YOU BECOME WHAT YOU CONSUME

A while back, I knew this guy who would always get angry after going to Walmart.

It was hilarious because for the most part, he was a calm dude.

But after Walmart, he was pissed off.

He died in a car accident.

In his funeral, his girlfriend tried to keep it light.

She noticed the same exact attribute about him.

She said:

'One day, I saw my boyfriend and he was mad. I was like... are you just getting back from Walmart?'

And the audience shared a warm laugh in the dark funeral.

I saw this friend yday who in my opinion has been becoming stranger by the day.

He posts a lot of controversial stuff on Instagram and Snapchat.

It's one thing to post it because you are trying to wake people up.

It's another thing to post it because you are trying to get a rise out of someone.

I view him as the latter.

He used to be a smart kid.

I still think he is.

However, he is so deep in the rabbit hole of conspiracy theories that nowadays he is just a negative dark dude.

Talking about Lucifer, the elite, how the world is ending etc.

Do I believe everything on the media?
Hell no.
Do I think a lot of conspiracy theories have some truth to it?
At times.

However, there needs to be a fine line regarding what you feed your mind.
Is it elevating you or leaving worse off?
Feeling disgusted.

Education is meant to make you feel 10 times taller so you have more potential to influence your future.
Education is not meant to make you feel oppressed, helpless, and lost.

A lot of smart people are using their phones to give themselves a panic attack.

Just like I knew this deceased friend came back from Walmart when I saw rage in his eyes.
Nowadays, I know people just got done scrolling when I see rage in their eyes.
The phone is just a tool.
You become what you consume.
There is no denying that.

Hopefully, when you're on your deathbed, you're happy with what you fed your mind.
And not thinking:
'Damn, I let impulses and the algorithm dictate my future...'

ONE WORD CAN CHANGE YOUR LIFE

I used to be a big fan of wrestling growing up.

There was a guy named Vince McMahon.
He changed how the wrestling business functions.

Earlier, he viewed his business as a, 'wrestling company.'
Who was his target market?

The target market was a bunch of single dudes who would come, buy beers, and would yell at the wrestlers to hurt each other.
These guys typically fell within the 40-year-old range.

Vince was not satisfied with his.
He believed he needed to change direction in order to make a splash with wrestling.

One day, he was brainstorming with his superstar Hulk Hogan.
Thinking....
Thinking some more.

Suddenly, he got an idea!

This was not a:

* Wrestling Company.

It was a:

- Wrestling ENTERTAINMENT Company.

When he had that idea, his body was ringing with sensations.
This was it.
This added word would change the direction of wrestling *forever*.

Now Hulk Hogan was not just a brute.
Instead, he was Mickey Mouse.
While Vince was Walt Disney.

The product was not found behind the blood.
It was found behind the drama.

Now Vince's target audience was not a bunch of single men looking to buy 1 ticket and multiple beers.
Instead, his target audience was a family unit.

Family of 4 perhaps?
Mom.
Dad.
Son.
Daughter.

The son and daughter would love to buy toys.
Shirts.
Possibly video games down the line.
So many opportunities!

The dots began connecting.
One word changed the **entire** direction.

POMPOUS QUESTIONS

Not everyone hates through statements.
Many hate through questions.

It's harder to spot the latter.

Sometimes, I'll watch an interview and see the journalist asking the question in a very sarcastic tone:
'Do you realllllyy think this?'

That's not a question, that's a bait.
Asking questions with an undertone of sarcasm will be perceived as disrespect.

Around 2017, Hurricane Irma was hitting Tampa.
It was begin branded as the:
-Hurricane of all Hurricanes.

So, my roommates and I boarded up our windows.
We were expecting a catastrophic disaster.

After the hurricane, nothing bad happened to us.
Nothing happened at all!
We barely lost internet connection.

It took a **long** time boarding up the windows.
There was this annoying thorn bush we had to deal with while adding the wooden board to the living room window.

The roommates decided it would be best to wait a few days to take the boards off.

Plus, with the boarded windows, there was a nice shade.

It felt like a brand-new place!

The urgency reduced even more.

Soon, the boards went from being up for a few days to 2 weeks.

One day, there was this dude who was aggressively knocking on our door.

My roommate opened the door.

This guy was in his mid-50s.

Big beard.

Average built, probably went to the gym twice a month.

He looked at my roommate first and me second.

(I was sitting at my desk that you can see once the door is opened).

This man angrily asks:

'You still haven't taken the boards off yet?'

My roommate was like:

'Who the fuck are you?'

I've never seen this man in my life.

Who is he to talk to us like that?

He said:

'You guys should have taken the boards off by now.'

My roommate said:
'We'll take the boards off when we feel like it.'

The guy then said that he was the president of the homeowner's association.

And he **'expected'** us to take the boards off asap.

Then he left.

That moment caught us both off-guard.

We decided this was a man of authority.

We better take the boards off soon.

What I recall from that moment was the level of aggression he came in with.

The question was fair.

The tone was not.

I used to think tone was overrated.

However, once I started creating content, I realized that tone influences perception.

The tone someone communicates with will determine how quickly the message is received.

Every now and then, power plays do speed up the process.

Like stating that you're the president of the homeowner's association.

But often, power plays are not needed if the question was asked in a curious way.

Anyways, I don't know what that dude went through before.

He probably had other people who didn't take their boards off either and was pissed by the time he came to our house.

The main takeaway is that questions can open up a lot of doors.

But can close a lot of doors too.

HOW TO SPOT STREET SMARTS

Without getting too technical, I want to tell you a story about street smarts.
It should symbolize that there is a time & place for logic.

A couple of years back, I was a fresh faced youngster starting my first internship.
It was going to be in an Aerospace company

I was going to be working as the systems engineer under a guy named John D'Brot.
He seemed like he was a few years older than me.

Imagine my surprise when I found out he was 45.

I saw the amount of stress that John went through.
But it wasn't always like that.

In the beginning of my hiring, I didn't respect John that much.
Thought he wasn't technical enough.

He was always running around working with different team members.
Talking a lot, but not coding a lot.

I spent most of my time dealing with this fellow named Hoa.
A Chinese man who looked even younger than me.
Hoa loved to talk.

I respected Hoa because he was technical.
He knew the nitty gritty details of a system, knew the infrastructure used to design it, and knew how to code!

That's what a *real* engineer did.

As more time went on by, John wanted me to move around in the team.
His goal was to give me the most experience as possible, so next year, the company could hire me full time.

He had me sitting with guys like Hoa, software engineers like
Amy & hardware technicians like Jean.

As I interreacted with these different members, I noticed
something.
'What?'
They all respected John.

Even though John wasn't the most technical, he was technical
enough.

He knew how each team operated from a high level overview.
And it was John that was having the tough meetings with the
clients.

One day, a conflict occurred...

Our team wanted to use a battery to power up a circuit.
While the clients were ADAMANT that we used a capacitor.
They wanted a cheaper price, so the capacitator seemed like a no
brainer.

Only problem was that this fix would require much more time.
And that's not what our team was expecting.

Our goal was to have John verbalize that a capacitor was simply
not possible.
IT HAD TO BE A BATTERY ONLY CIRCUIT.

In that meeting, John confidently said:
'No, we will do as the client says' with a smile on his face.

The rest of the team fought back.
But John did not budge.

He said that we needed to get back to work and make the
changes.
The team continued to fight back.
But John did not budge....

Later that week, as I visited the different team members, I
noticed how the tune had changed.

Amy, Hoa, Jean were all talking shit about John.
They said he was a pushover & didn't have guts.

It was fascinating to see how quickly everyone turned on him.
I was a rookie, so I didn't say much.
Just listened & kept out of the shit talking.

The next week, John invites me to his office for a 1 hour meeting.

Hmm....
Strange.

Normally, John was quick and to the point.
A 1 hour meeting was 45 minutes beyond his typical meetings.

In the email, he wrote:
'Bring lunch with you.'

THE DAY OF OUR MEETING ARRIVED.

I went to his office with my hot dogs & Capri sun.
He was eating his wife's pasta & drinking a diet coke.

That's when John and I spoke....

'You know Armani. You came in a very tumultuous time in the company. Our company is getting bought out. Scott, the president of the company, is getting fired next week. Things are changing. A new management is in town.'

Wait, what???

'In times of change, we need to adjust. Those who cannot adjust will fall behind Armani. Sometimes, a leader has to make a decision that will not make everyone happy. But it is for the greater good.'

The more I spoke to John in that meeting, the more I saw EXACTLY why he decided to switch the trajectory of our project.

John had street smarts.

He knew that there was a time & place for logic.

Logically, us changing the trajectory of our project did not make
sense.
Not only would the circuit be less effective, it would take us
longer.

Emotionally, John saw the bigger picture.
He had intel of our company being bought out.
He was operating with more information than the people talking
shit about him.

He realized that the clients who we were dealing with were
stubborn.
It was a 'their way or the high way' kind of mentality.

He also knew that he could keep twisting their arm to get his way.
But at this point, the risk was not worth it.

Had we lost that client, the people who were talking shit about
John may have gotten fired.
The new management who bought out our company were
ITCHING to fire people.

Since they were new, they didn't have emotional ties with the
employees. They just saw money in vs money out.

John took one for the team.
He put his reputation on the line for the greater good.
Temporarily though.

Over time, we saw what John was doing.
Once the project was done, the clients were happy.

But the clients were able to see FIRST HAND that the
suggestions they requested were suboptimal.

So they came back with their tail between their legs asking for the
battery pack version.

John was 5 steps ahead.
Guess what the client requesting changes meant?
'What??'

Repeat business.

Repeat business for a small aerospace company is very good.
It allowed our team to show the new management that our
department meant business.

It was John, who was the captain.

He was the leader who taught me that technical skills without
street smarts will have you looking like a dummy..

One common phrase I hear tossed around is the 'Starving Artist.'
The creative fellow with o business acumen.

Another phrase I'd like to coin is the 'Awkward Worm.'
The book worm with o street smarts.

They view the world so much through logic, that they fail to
understand that logic alone cannot solve problems that involves
humans.

The higher someone rises, the more street smarts are needed.
More John's are needed who can maintain their cool when their
back is against the wall.

His team is turning on him.
His client's are talking down to him.

Yet, he has that cool, calm demeanor which makes you think:
'Everything will be okay.'

John is the person who will rise.
The rest will work for him.

Technical or not, a leader knows how to command people.
And knows how to see that the world filled with boundaries
have **plenty** of loopholes.

THE SHOCK OF HEARING YOUR VOICE

I don't want to be that guy.
But I will be.

Back in my days.....
Our smartphones could only record videos up to 8-10 seconds long.

Due to the small duration of the video clips, my friends and I mainly took videos of things around us.
Parties, scenery, school fights.
You know...the usual.

As I started to grow up, the technology became more advanced.
Now the phone camera's could record longer videos.

Rather than pointing the camera outwards, now we pointed it towards us.

One of the first times I mindfully heard myself talking on tape was in my senior year of college.
Was very surprised by how I sounded.

Hated it to be honest.

A few years later, when I joined Toastmasters, the club I was a part of would record the speakers.
This allowed the speakers to review the tapes later & get a different perspective.

Once again, I hated it.

The advancement of technology was bringing me into eye contact with how I sounded.

As I started to grow up even more, I saw others coming in eye contact with the same issue.
They were mortified hearing themselves on tape.

They put the headphones in their ears, hit the play button, and thought:

'This is how I sound??? What a flat voice I have... What a boring voice I have...What a nasally voice I have!!'

Back in my days, you could've easily ran away from this issue.

You didn't necessarily NEED to hear yourself on tape.
That was something that you would do on your own volition.

But nowadays?
There is less hiding.

Speaking on tape & hearing your voice is spilling over to the corporate and entrepreneurial worlds.

-Tons of individuals in corporations are being called to do training videos which will be recorded.

-Tons of entrepreneurs have to create promo videos sharing their brand mission.

Nowadays, more people have to come in contact with how they sound.

'What did you learn from all this Armani?'
I learned there are 3 stages of hearing your voice.

Stage 1: Shock

You may be going through this right now.
I don't use the word 'shock' lightly.

However you think I am using it...multiply it by 10.
Others will not tell you, but they are *mortified* when they hear themselves talking.

Completely normal.
Understand this stage exists.

Stage 2: Acceptance

This is a stage that some will never reach.
The shock from stage 1 is so strong, that they will continue to make excuses forever.

They will die with their excuses.
Lost potential & lost opportunities to rise in their field.

To reach acceptance, there needs to be an UNDERSTANDING of how the voice works.

Right now, you think the voice is some random blob.
You're not quite sure what it is.

Learn about the voice and the 4 components within it.
Breath, vocal chords, resonators and articulators.

When you learn about the voice, you'll be fascinated how many variables are moving for you to say something as simple as 'apple.'

In addition to that, be grateful that you HAVE a voice.
'Why would I be grateful for that? Doesn't everyone have a voice?'
No.

There are tons of people who cannot speak.

And if they can, they have a thing called 'vocal paralysis,' which makes them hard to hear.

Be grateful that you don't have these issues.
By submerging yourself in the darkness of what exists, you become more exposed to the light.

Stage 3: Acceptance and Dissatisfaction

There's a myth that people with a great voice love their voice.
Not true.

I think one of the greatest voices I ever heard was from my old school public speaking mentor, Joe Yazbeck.

He is a world renowned speaker, former Broadway actor, and singer too!

I found out around the end of our training that he doesn't love his voice.
He keeps on loving it.

Stage 2 should give you acceptance for your voice.
This allows you to feel gratitude that you have a voice at all.

But in stage 3, we don't just want acceptance.
We want strategic dissatisfaction.

'Why would I want to be dissatisfied for??'
Because this allows you to experiment.
'Experiment what?'

Experiment with:
-The different tonalities that you possess.
-The different ways you can bend a word.
-The different melodies of your voice.

The voice is a musical instrument that keeps on giving

Do you think a famous musician is like:
'I know how to play the piano, guess I have nothing else to learn.'

Of course not!
The pianist (loll I always laugh at that word) continues to learn more about that piano.

They continue to use their past lessons to experiment more and create lessons for the future.

Plenty of individuals stop at Stage 1.
They will never get over the shock.

Hopefully, if you're reading this, you are ready to push forward in your journey.

To learn how to tackle Stage 2 & 3 with grace, check out the Speak Easy book.

This book covers:

-How to put thoughts into words so you can express yourself clearly & concisely.

-How to create an articulation chamber so you can take your voice to the gym & sound more confident.

-How to use your voice to create professional opportunities & make more money.

CRAWL BEFORE YOU CAN WALK

Seeing a baby learn how to walk is fascinating.
The rise of something new.

You can tell the pressure they feel.
Learning the art of balancing.
Controlling the mind.
Then gathering their body to move forward.

They fall.
-Then get back up.
They fall.
-Then get back up.
They fall.
-And get back up without hesitation.

The baby has the mindset of a victor.
What I'm describing with this toddler can be applied in the game
of life.

The School of Hard Knocks.

This baby one day becomes an adult.
The memory of them fumbling & stumbling is of the distant past.

They are now looking at a new generation of babies....
Falling & getting back up.

This is the concept of not skipping the process.
And doing your best to remember your roots.

No matter which skillset it is, know that it's easy to get
brainwashed nowadays.

-Seeing people's end products rather than their process.
-Seeing how others are walking, rather than how they were once
falling.

Whichever skillset that you are in the process of mastering, be
like that baby.

Fall & get back up without hesitation.

Crawl before you can walk.
Walk before you can run.
Run before you can fly.

If you are currently aiming to grow in the field of
communication...
More specifically, you're learning to speak in front of a camera.
I give you a 1 minute pep talk in this following video.

Don't quit yet!
Keep going, record your videos & have the guts to hit publish.

24/7 INSPIRATION

Have you ever wondered what was the purpose of practicing?

There are different definitions for it.
The definitions are influenced by the field being practiced.

With communication skills, we are playing a mental sport.
A mental sport is different than a physical sport.

A physical sport is more susceptible to natural laws.
Tom Brady retired today.

He was one of the rare physical athletes who defied natural laws.
If you ever heard him talk, he loved the game of Football. He often talked about playing till 50 years old.

Play until 50?
What, you trying to overcome father time??

He got close.
At the time of his retirement, he stands at 44 years old.

However, he even had to hang it up.
He plays a physical sport and understands that his body cannot over some laws.

On the other hand, mental sports are not susceptible to the same laws.

A young adult can write stories well into their 50s.

Heck, you can argue they'll write their BEST stories in their 50s+!

Mainly because they have more life experience & have gotten a massive head start in articulating their ideas.

Therefore, with communication skills, we need to have a longer scope of reality.

In terms of practicing, the goal is to *become infinite*.

Infinite in terms of an expanded decision tree.

When I first started my podcast in 2019, I thought there were only a few topics to talk about.

How many episodes can I really do on soft skills?

300+ episodes later, I realized... plenty.

Also, I learned the same thing in terms of the voice.

Before, I thought the voice mainly comes down to loud or soft.

A micro change registers as something completely new.

When you record a podcast, you get a staticky graph.

I saw after 300 episodes, that no 2 graphs will ever be the same.

If I talk about even a small twist to a similar topic,
the **meaning** in the graph will be different.

It's sort of like a thumb print: content edition.

There are 2 possible problems that a mental athlete will face:

1. Lack of ideas.

2. Not enough time to articulate all ideas.

Both are problems.

The question is, which problem do you want?

I used to think that I would struggle with 1.

Didn't even think problem 2 was a thing.

Nowadays, my paradigm has flipped.

I can't think how anyone can have a problem with #1.

It seems logically impossible to have a problem with #1.

The mind has ~30,000 thoughts per day.

How is it that the user of the mind can't string together at least 100 of those thoughts to form a quick talk??

It's not a content issue.

It's a concentration issue.

Chances are the person does not practice creativity.

Which is why they don't perceive themselves to be creative.

It's like an athlete who only shows up to the game...and they suck.

They wonder why.

So, they ask their coach.

The coach is like:

'Because you never come to practice!!!'

Physical and mental sports have one thing in common:
Practice is a must.

The more we practice, the more we perceive the:

-MICRO shifts in body movements.

-MICRO evolution of our ideas.

 -MICRO evolution of our voice.

Only the mental superstars will perceive that transition.

It's because the mental superstars practiced articulating their ideas over and over again....

EDUCATION BASED MARKETING

I'm not too sure how you found me.
Before, I thought I would've known.

I used to think everyone who is on this list found me through my
Twitter account.
They saw my tweets, found a promo for my email list & boom..
Signed up.

My perception changed on multiple occasions.
I realized different people on this list discovered me in different
ways.

One story was pretty fascinating.
I wonder if he is reading this right now...

In undergrad, I pledged a fraternity.
During my pledging process, I wanted to learn **everything** about
the fraternity.

I wanted to know when it was founded, the founding fathers,
what the fraternity stands for.
All that.

I realized how passionate a lot of the brothers were.
(Brothers are the titles for the fraternity members).

'So how did you like the Frat?'
Whoa...you made a mistake, my friend.
'What?'
You called it a Frat.

I once called it a Frat during a recruiting event. I wasn't a
member then.
That's when a brother corrected me and said:
*'Don't call a Fraternity a Frat, Armani. You wouldn't like it if I
called your Country a Cunt. Would you?'*

I laughed when he said that.
He was being serious.

I respected him for telling me this.
He took his organization seriously.

I like people who represent things with pride.
Even if I disagree with it....if you're going to work, do it with some effort.

I studied with effort.

Memorized the names of the founding fathers.
This was over a decade ago.
However, the names are still etched in my subconscious mind.

Imagine my surprise when one of the founding father's emails me and says:
'Yo ArmaniTalks! I am one of your fraternity brothers. I just discovered your website & bought your book. I like what you're doing. Keep it up.'

This seems like a small comment.
But it was meaningful moment for me.

My younger self kept hearing & reciting their names.
I wanted to show that I knew the history of the organization that I was joining.

Now one of the members who **created** the whole organization was reaching out to me.

I view marketing as a powerful force.
I view education as a powerful force.

When I started ArmaniTalks, I did not do it for fame.
Don't care about that.
My goal is the opposite.

If no one knew me & I could keep doing what I do, I'd prefer that.
However, that's not realistic.

The core of the business is this list.
Behind the scenes work.

It's the education that brings others to this list.
Some found me through twitter.
Some found me through a YouTube video.
Some found me through a blog.

The way this Fraternity brother found me was through a book.
I had a friend who interviewed me for a book & I was on the first chapter.

This showed me a few lessons regarding marketing on the internet.
If you can view promotion as educating, there is a tension free process created from that.

A cool, calm, collected composure is built.

My brother was in sales for over 3 years.
He was top tier in his field.

Even for him, he didn't like 'selling' before.
For some reason, the phrase didn't sit well with him.

Well, how did he go from the state of uneasiness to dominating later on?
He understood his version of 'sales.'

He said he educated others.

This allowed him to feel like he was doing others a favor rather than taking something from them.
It was easier to close at that point.

In this era, self promotion is only sleazy if you think that's the only kind of promotion there is.

But if you can have SOME SORT of education based marketing into your mix, that's when the tension melts.

It doesn't matter what field you are in.
Plumbing, engineering, writing etc.
Aim to teach.

Teaching is one of the noblest fields out there.

It's like you are walking in the dark room of someone's mind &
turning the light on.

**That ON light will never allow them to view life the same
way again.**
That's my intention with this newsletter.

Are you sitting & observing others participate?
Or are you participating yourself?

Teaching is an honorable field.
Not one that you study from the outside.
But one that you bring alive from the inside.

Step into the arena.
Share your knowledge, skills & expertise.

ENTREPRENEURIAL LONELINESS

Entrepreneurship is not a profession.
Entrepreneurship is a mindset.

'What does this mindset entail, Armani?'
A few things.

-Curiosity
-Problem solving mentality (remember this one for later)
-Ability to build
-Turn ideas into reality
-Desire for more

An entrepreneur is a businessman plus an artist.

'Why did you title this talk, entrepreneurial loneliness?'
Because this mindset can get lonely.

Loneliness is not physical.
It's mental.

If you are surrounded by 100 people who you do not connect
with, then you'll feel lonely.
If you are surrounded by 1 person who you do connect with, then
you won't feel lonely.

That 1 person should always be you, first.
Otherwise, loneliness is on the horizon.
It's just a matter of time.

The entrepreneur's mindset is rare.
You can say it is the awakened mind in the land of the blind.

Sleepwalking through life is a real thing.

'What is your definition of sleepwalking through life?'
Good question.
It's when your future is simply a repetition of your past.

This is a mind that is not waking up.

A person who sleepwalks through life mentally faces backward, while physically walking forward.

But the entrepreneurial mind is vastly differently.
They use their past as learning lessons.
And their future can be entirely different.

-It's impossible to predict the behavior of an entrepreneur.
-It's possible to predict the behavior of a person who sleepwalks through life.

Rarity can cause loneliness.
No matter how gifted that rare person is.

This is why I am a big fan of email newsletters.
'Why?'
Because it can build a connection.

Yes, building friends in the real world is a thing.
But let's imagine you live in the middle of nowhere.

Right now, most people in your community probably behaves the same.
Same rituals, cultural beliefs & friend groups.

How is an entrepreneurial mind supposed to find a connection there?
Considering how rare the mind is...

That's when you go GLOBAL.
Global can turn a rare occasion into a norm.

With newsletters, you can connect with someone on a global level.
It's even better when they speak your mind for you.

I'm a part of a few newsletters.
There's one guy I read all the time.
But he's not consistent.

He posts every now and then.
When he does post, I feel like he is talking to **me.**

His writing style is conversational.
Easy to understand & easier to relate to.

I'm thinking:
'Man, you should post more often!'

He's not consistent because his focus is on other endeavors.
All good, I look forward to those rare occasions.

That's a reason I post on this newsletter everyday.
I like to connect with the people who open **every** email.

'There are people who open every email? Don't daily emails
annoy others???'
-It annoys people who do not connect with me like that.
-It does not annoy people who do connect with me like that.

It's because people who read every day are the ones who resonate
with me.
A part of my writing puts their thoughts into words.

Use newsletters to help with entrepreneurial loneliness.
This may seem like a unique solution, but it's not.
It's just one of many suggestions.

Another suggestion is to join a local BNI (Business Networking
International) club.
Or any business networking club near you.

I used to be the Communications Chair for my BNI chapter and
met a lot of great people.
People who I still talk to.
People who are on this newsletter.

If you're an entrepreneurial mind, then you'll figure it out.
Remember one of the traits I listed on the top?

You're a problem solver.

A true problem solver thrives in moments when their back is
against the wall.
When they feel sad... they turn it into creativity.

An entrepreneur is the only mindset that can perform alchemy at will.
So I'm sure you'll get through this moment with grace.

If you have other entrepreneurial friends, let them know about my newsletter.

Friends remember friends who recommend them information that is suited to their personal needs.

WHY YOU DON'T FEEL CONFIDENT

With blurriness comes uncertainty.
With uncertainty comes fear.

Let me ask you a question.
'Shoot!'
Do you know how you look?
'What kind of dumb question is that? Of course I know how I look!'
I don't think you do.

It's easy to overestimate how well we THINK we know how we look.
But in reality, it's not always that clear.

It's easy to spot who we are in a group picture.
However, when closing the eyes, the mind struggles to recreate our image.

Struggling to recreate ourselves creates blurriness.
With blurriness comes uncertainty.
That uncertainty leads to self esteem issues.

I'm breaking down why the Illusion of Transparency exists.
This is when you think your internal nerves are leaking out to the public.

The illusion of transparency is the cause of social anxiety & speech anxiety.

At a root level, all this can be traced back to having a fuzzy idea of how our face looks.

You can't blame us either.
We spend life in 1st perspective mode.
Not 3rd.

Luckily, modern information technology gave us power to flip that.
Nowadays, we can record a quick clip of us & see ourselves.

It's one thing when you see yourself in a mirror.
It's another thing when you see yourself in video.

The mirror gets you introverted & thinking.
The video allows you to see yourself as another entity.

This is tip #20 in my new blog:
 "20 Tips on How to Improve Your Self Esteem."

It doesn't matter how gifted you are if you don't think you are gifted.
Your self esteem is the narrative of your thoughts.

In this Mega Blog Post, you'll be given a lot of innovative ideas to improve your inner dialogue.

Think powerful thoughts, practice hard & influence others.
If you like this, it'll help me out if you can share it on your social media of choice!

UNPOPULAR OPINION

When I was younger, I recall going to Applebee's a lot with my family.

I'd get the steak and double mashed potatoes all the time.

That was the go-to, of course!

One time, we went to Applebee's and there was a Haitian family that sat next to us.

The father was black, bald, and had a moustache.

The mom had long hair and thick Harry Potter glasses.

And the 2 boys were roughly 12 and 15 years-old with dreads.

The 2 boys ordered burgers.

I recall hearing the waitress and how she was talking to the family.

Very rude.

Rarely asking them if they needed water.

Sighed when being asked for ranch and buffalo sauce.

Had this sharp condescending tone.

It was awkward.

Earlier, I heard the dad talking.

He was talking about how he had a rough couple of months in his business.

And now it was time to celebrate.

He finally got a win after a long time.

Before the 2 boys ordered, he said:
'Order whatever.'

I thought that was funny because my dad would always say the same thing as well:
'Order whatever.'

The family wasn't **always** going to Applebee's to eat.
Instead, they went when there was a special occasion.
Now this rude waitress was ruining the experience.

One quote I hear a lot is:
'Always judge people based off how they treat the staff.'

Then every now and then, someone gets exposed for talking to the staff rudely.
In the common section, there are a bunch of people with a common sentiment.
The person who talked rudely to the staff is a piece of shit that should be looked at as a 2nd class citizen.

They justify their logic by saying:
'Maybe the staff was having a poor day.'

That's when I think of that family, and I'm like:
*'Maybe the customer was having a bad **month**.'*

If that family returned rudeness back to that waitress, I wouldn't have thought any less of them.

Is it worth it?

Nah.

But I don't view humans as perfect creatures.

I view them as flawed creatures with pride, narratives, and emotions.

Ones that will retaliate when they feel like they are being treated unfairly.

It's very easy to get carried away with emotional intelligence.

An example is when society allows people to bring their mood to work with them.

That's when professionalism melts away.

When professionalism melts away, that's when a lot of things we take for granted begin to melt away as well.

I had this Applebee's memory recently as I was about to get my haircut.

I get a lot of anxiety before getting a haircut.

A while back, I used to go to this very expensive place.

They'd do some little snips and I was done.

60 bucks.

I thought.

'Hm...They are barely doing that much work. My haircut is very simple. Maybe I should go to a cheaper place that charges 20 bucks.'

So, that's what I did.

When I went to the 20 bucks place, I saw a different problem.
The quality was poor.

I got a haircut recently by a sweet middle-aged woman.
She boasted about how she had been cutting hair for years.
She was respectful and had good conversational skills.

But the haircut she gave was subpar to awful.
Very jaggedy and uneven hair.

I normally don't like to tell the barber to fix stuff, but it was bad enough for me to say:
'You missed this spot.'

I pulled out a segment of hair which was completely untouched.
Then she said:
'Oh, sorry.'

Slowly, this service became a participatory project.

I was guiding her.
And she causally did as she was told.

Eventually, it became annoying.
I said it was okay.
Paid her and gave her a tip.

I came home and finished her job for her.
Snips away.

Poor quality service leads to more problems than answers.

Emotional intelligence done wrong is asking:

'Well, how can we empathize with the poor server, so we make sure that we don't offend them?'

The first half of that question is not flawed.

I had to empathize with the poor barber.

I realized she cuts a lot of heads a day.

Eventually, she went from seeing details to the holistic version of the hair.

It's like a storyteller who focuses on the overall story versus every last spelling.

Both are important; however, at times, the little details get away.

The second part of the question is flawed.

Offending is not always bad.

It should be a last case scenario.

But every now and then, it is warranted.

Offensive words serve as a feedback for better behavior.

It's not up to the customer to reduce their standards to meet an organizations emotions.

It's up to the organization to deliver quality processes, products, and service to satisfy the customer.

If a rude customer comes along, then handle them on a case by case basis.

But a customer should not be asked to tolerate rude service.
Poor quality work and carelessness is a form of rudeness.

The problem with the economy is that we don't have enough artists.
Enough craftsmen.

A craftsman doesn't bring their attitude to their profession.
They don't need to be guided by the patron on how to do their job.

Instead, there is a raw desire to improve and keep getting better.

Think like that as the leader of an organization or profession.
-How can I create more artists?
-How can I become an artist myself?

People need less handouts and pats on the back.
They need more perspective.

It's not always about the individual nodes.
It's about bringing value to society whether you feel like it or not.
That's emotional intelligence done the right way.

FROM THE HORSE'S MOUTH

'From the horse's mouth' is a figure of expression which is defined as:

-Hearing from the person directly concerned or another authoritative source.

This concept is more important than ever.

There are 2 reasons why.

- One reason is due to how easy it is to edit.
- Second reason is because a lot of 'subject matter experts' do not know what they are talking about.

For reason one, editing is a lot like coding.

Back in the days, if you were going to code, you needed punch cards.

It was a highly manual process.

But as tech improved, it became easier to debug code.

Back in the days, a lot of editors used scissors.

They would collect the film.

And if they needed to make adjustments, then there would be people with scissors snipping away.

Nowadays?

It's easy to edit.

You just click Control B and delete.

Since it's so easy to edit, it's easier than ever to take people out of context.

That is what a lot of sinister people do.

They chop away pieces of content to present a distorted message to the masses that sparks a reaction.

So if you see someone you trust being presented in a negative light...

Rather than taking the snippet alone at face value, it's best to hear it from the horse's mouth.

-What were they really trying to say?

The distortion doesn't only happen with content.

The distortion also happens with gossip.

'Joey was talking shit about me?? I just gave him a ride to the airport. Ungrateful bastard.'

Before taking Lucy's word at face value.

Best to hear from Joey before cutting ties.

The second reason to hear from the horse's mouth is because a lot of ignorant people are vocal.

Many learn just to show off how 'smart' they are.

But they are in no position to be teaching.

They barely grasp the fundamentals.

There was one time I was listening to a podcast.

There was a girl on the show who was talking about the Vedas.

She was talking about how the Vedas are a story that was created by a few people.

She was delivering her statements with the utmost confidence.

The person I was watching it with was **furious**.

The furious person studied the Vedas for a while.

And this person was like:

'This girl on the show has no clue what the Vedas are!'

A lot of ideas are not grasped at the fundamental root.

Yet, the person is over here speaking about it.

This person is vocal.

And often, this person is heavily biased.

There have been a few times I was like:

'That idea? Nah, I wouldn't ever rock with that idea. Johannes told me that idea was whack.'

But was Johannes well equipped to teach me about that idea?

In this case, going to the horse's mouth is studying about the idea that got a reaction out of me before forming an opinion.

This is easy in theory, but **very difficult** to do.

Wise individuals learn how NOT to have an opinion.

That doesn't mean they won't ever have an opinion on the matter (or it may mean exactly that).

But it means that in a world of misinformation, biases, and lies...

They're waiting to understand rather than just have an opinion
for the sake of having an opinion.

They think:

*'Let me know what I'm talking about. Otherwise, I'm going to
hear it from the horse's mouth before making any rash
judgments.'*

GOOD KIND VS BAD KIND

One time, I was sent to New Jersey for training.

I was given a card.

This card had money in it.

When I arrived in New Jersey, there were people from all over the US that were attending.

People from California, Houston, Florida and more.

Later, the trainees discovered that those who lived far away from New Jersey got **way more** money in their card than people who lived close to New Jersey.

For example: the California and Florida trainees received a higher amount in their cards vs the Delaware and New York trainees.

Eventually word got out of how much the money discrepancy was.

A lot of the poorly compensated trainees were furious.

After training, we would often go to have dinner and occasionally go to a bar.

Since the California and Florida people had way more money, we would often treat others.

There was this Asian girl named Kim.

She was around 5'2, shy, and brown haired.

She was one of trainees who felt that the money discrepancy was unjust!

She lived in Delaware.

And Kim complained to the other trainees about the Floridians and Californians.

What I found amusing about Kim was that she wasn't complaining when the Floridians and Californians were buying the food and drinks.

Heck, she would invite strangers and order on their behalf!

She would be like:

'What's your name again? Sally? Sally, come and join us. Of course, you can order whatever on the menu!'

To strangers, Kim was one of the kindest people out there.

To me, Kim was one of the kindest people out there... with other people's money!

That's the fake kind of kind.

Where you use other people's resources to show what a good-hearted person you are.

That doesn't require much work.

It mainly requires intention alone.

'Well, isn't intent what mainly matters when giving?'

To a certain extent, yes.

There are people who are the flipside of Kim but not too far off.

They have the resources.

But they are not good with their intent.
They mainly give to be like:
'Watch me. I'm the man.'

This person has the resources.
But their intent is questionable.

No one can fully be certain of someone else's intent.
It's pure speculation.
Only the giver knows.

But one crucial question I ask is:
'Are you putting your money where your mouth is...to the best of your abilities?'

Everyone doesn't have money.
But they have time.
Are they atleast attending the meetings with their time?

It's difficult to distinguish good kind from bad kind.

But if I see someone at least putting their own resources up, then the optics look infinitely better than Kim ordering food with other people's money...
Then complaining about the same people she took money from.

'What are your thoughts on bragging after giving? Does that negate the act of kindness?'
It depends.

I have no problem with occasional bragging.

Different people brag for different reasons:

1. Some have sinister motives.
2. Some have self esteem issues.
3. And others are bragging because they put in **a lot** of effort.

Most of their effort is not being seen.

Just like you see 1/9th of an iceberg.

You're seeing 1/9th of their effort in relation to this activity.

For this group who put in an immense effort, I'm here for it!

Talk yo' shit!

Of course, there is decorum.

Bragging nonstop is in poor taste.

But when a feat was gargantuan, an occasional brag doesn't seem to negate the purity of the act, in my opinion.

"Did you know this is the first ever turkey handout we had in this neighborhood for Thanksgiving? I had to raise 100,000$ from local investors. A record high."

Sometimes, what's viewed as bragging by one person is another person stating facts.

I've often seen a lot of people adopt the 'oh shucks,' mentality.

Where they are trying to be liked so much that they undermine any effort they put in.

'Who me? No, I didn't do ANYTHING!'

This seems more disingenuous than letting an occasional human behavior slip out.

I'm not condoning bragging by the way.

But when evaluating humans, I found that the best perspective is to view them as illogical creatures prior to viewing them as logical creatures.

When you view humans through logic alone, their actions make little sense.

When you view humans from an illogical lens, their actions make more sense.

Recap time.

If you're going to be kind, cool!

At least put up your own resources (to the best of your abilities).

If you put up your own resources, then the optics look great.

However, the intent is only something that you are aware of.

If Person X put their own resources up and did a kind act...

Then Person X begins bragging.

Their bragging may cause you to completely negate the value of the act that they just did.

But before questioning their motive, view Person X as an illogical creature before a logical creature.

Then it will be easier to assess if their bragging was in poor faith or not.

LEAVE THE EXCUSES
AT THE DOOR

I woke up in the morning.
And my head was hurting.
Mouth was dry.
Felt fatigue as hell.

This was around 2016.

No clue what happened.
I was feeling great the night before.
Why am I suddenly sick?

To make matters worse, I had a speech coming up at my
Toastmasters club.

I woke up at 7am.
My speech was at 7pm.

This may be a big problem.
I could barely get out of bed.

I don't know what's worse.
The fact that I had to drive to work in this cold weather...
Or that I had to give a talk with this heated body.

Wait a minute.
Cold weather?

I felt the breeze in my room.
And it's freezing in my room.
The AC is **blasting** cold air.

Dammit!
My roommate left the AC on.
That may explain why I woke up feeling like this.

All my sick days were used up in work that year.
So I didn't want to burn good graces with my boss.

Decided to go to work.

As I am driving to work, I call my Toastmasters club president to let her know how sick I feel.
Asked her if it was too late to drop out as a speaker.

It was...

The other 2 speakers apparently had gotten sick too.
And they dropped out.
If I chose to join them, then there would be no speakers for this meeting.

Okay.
Say no more.
Suck it up & give the speech.

I dragged through work & was having trouble thinking.
Had moments when I forgot what my speech was about.

Am I setting myself to look like an idiot?
What if I get on stage & forget the whole talk?

Hours went on by & 7 pm was rolling around.

After drinking a lot of water & eating fruit, it was finally time to go into the meeting.

It was an average sized meeting.
25 people.
Everyone had their jackets on.

Our club meeting was hosted in a place with a lot of windows, so we could see the outside scenery.
It was the time of the day where the sun was going down.

I don't know why, but when it got dark like that outside, something about the room felt more friendly.
It felt like these strangers were now family.

As I was about to get on stage, the president stared at me from her chair.
She gave me the look like 'are you ready?'

I nodded my head.

Soon as I get on stage, I pulled the podium back.
There was always this annoying podium that stood there center stage.

My public speaking style is not to stand behind a podium.
I like to used the stage.

After pulling this heavy podium back...
I began my talk.

Opened with how I am feeling under the weather and then began my speech.

The talk was about fear.
I told a story about how one of my cousins pushed me into the swimming pool when I was a little kid, causing me to almost drown.

After that near death moment, my dad taught me the art of swimming.
The story was about how I overcame the fear of the pool.

Once the talk was done, I got a round of applause & the meeting continued.

Eventually, the evaluator was up.
This is the guy who breaks down what I did well in the talk and what could have been improved.

He was this Toastmasters veteran named Frank.
Frank was known for his brutally honest truths.

I was expecting him to shred my speech apart.
But surprisingly, he didn't.

He talked about how he enjoyed the story which set up the lesson.
F. E. A. R.
Face
Everything
And

Rise

He loved the unique path towards the lesson and said he learned a lot.
Frank also said my speech would help a lot of the new members give their first talk.

As he is talking me up, his tone suddenly changes....
Now he was about to share what could have been improved.

He said:
'Armani, you opened your speech saying how you were sick. Raise your hand if you knew Armani was sick before he bought it up.'

No one in the audience raised their hands.

'You see Armani? No one knew you were sick until you bought it up. If I were to improve one thing for your talk, it would be the opener. Never open with an excuse.'

That was a monumental moment for me.
And shifted how I viewed public speaking.

This had a lot of lessons regarding a speech & regarding life in general.

The lesson regarding speaking is that others can rarely tell what setbacks you are going through.

I felt like a mess.
And I even looked like a mess.
How could these people not tell?

To take it a level further, let's say they were able to tell.
What then?
Am I allowed to make the excuse then?

Nope.

Still, it's a game of the public speaker having a better opener than an excuse.

2 openers which should be avoided:

An excuse:
I am so sick, but oh well, here it goes.

Announced nervousness:
I am soo nervous, oh my! But oh well, here it goes.

When the speaker gets on stage, it's a game of spending those 7-10 minutes (the standard Toastmasters speech time) to rock the stage.

If you are looking for an opener, a few simple ones are:

1. Raise your hand if you like dogs more than cats.
Any 'if' condition that relates to the speech.

2. Another great opener is a shocking statistic that relates to the theme of the talk.

Learning that others couldn't tell I was sick shed tons of insights regarding speech anxiety.

Just like plenty of people could not tell I was sick, likewise, plenty of people cannot tell when you are nervous.

They are straight up oblivious.

Even though your inner world is falling apart.
The audience is viewing a different reality.
(Unless you're so nervous where you are physically shaking. Which surprisingly, is rare).

That day, Frank showed me that first impressions do matter.

But unlike popular belief, first impressions won't destroy you though.
Even though my opener was shaky, the rest of the speech made up for that.

So an opener is not something you want to sweat over day and night.

However, it serves as a cherry on top to a speech which has already been prepared for.
It's a way of showing the audience that now the speaker is in charge.

Those 7-10 minutes are the speaker's moments.
No backups or anything.

Public speaking is a modern day gladiator's sport.
Just like a boxer can only fight for himself.
A speaker can only use his or her words for themselves.

For those 7-10 minutes, the speaker is not sick.
Scared.
Or lazy.

For those 7-10 minutes, the speaker is the maestro.
Who conducts energy like copper.

And once those 7-10 minutes are up, now the speaker can once again feel the fever which was momentarily suspended.

WHAT DOES FREEDOM MEAN?

I often hear the phrase "freedom" getting thrown around.
It's a phrase that unites different groups of people.

-Entrepreneur's leave their jobs for freedom.
-Oppressed groups fight for their rights to gain more freedom.
-And societal norms are pushed to have more room to breathe.

Each of the groups above have a different definition for how they view the phrase.

In my opinion, one of my core staples of freedom comes down to 'saying whatever I want to say.'
Not in a malicious way.
Instead, in an explorative way.

That's one of the key staples of why I built this business in the first place.

Twitter, YouTube, blogs, podcasts etc.
I love those.
It gives me a chance to introduce new people to the ArmaniTalks brand.

But the heart of the business comes down to this email list.
It's where I don't have to play games with the algorithms & write about topics which are already being searched for.

Every now and then, I'll make a newsletter about a topic requested by one of my readers.
But that's not the norm.

The norm is for exploration in the sea of soft skills.

I think it's a bit ironic that a lot of business coaches never ask you what you want.
They immediately go to the tactics.

But how long can the tactics be executed when there is no underlying narrative?

Analogy time...
Let's say a plus sized man is trying on skinny pants.

Can it be done?
Sure.
But how long can this plus sized man keep sucking in his gut for?

Not long.

That's why when someone says they do what they do for freedom,
it is **always** more than the tactics.
It's more than something that is measurable.
It's subjective.

Saying whatever I want to say is my version of wearing the right
pants that fit. That's my kind of freedom.
However, the advice is not black and white.

Your idea of freedom can be something completely different.
Like having an office at work.

I had a coworker like that.
Ketan was his name.

One of the most charming guys on the floor.
He knew how to make you feel empowered.

Only problem?
He was very antisocial.

He had one of the biggest rooms on the floor.
Every now and then, he would come out to use the restroom.
Other than that, he would stay inside his office.
He'd eat lunch by himself.

Since Ketan was a man of power, others would come to his office.
They would come for meetings or just stop by to say hi.

I was working with Ketan for a small project.
We formed a small bond.

He is Indian and I am Bengali.

So our skin colors sped up the rapport.

During our interaction, he said that it was always his dream to
have a big office like the one he had.
He jokingly said:
'that's why I rarely leave it, haha.'

Not only was the office designed nicely.
It also smelled great.
He took care of it.

The office was more than a physical location that he worked in.
It was his symbol of freedom.

When I looked at the office, I saw a manager sitting in a
managerial room.

When Ketan saw the office, he saw:

-Moving from India to the US
-Taking a bet on himself
-Hard work & persistence
-A career that commanded respect
-A career that had others coming to him

And much more.

His definition of freedom is not 'being able to say whatever he
wants to say' like mine is.
For him, it's about having a piece of real estate that he can call his
own.

His kids aren't bugging him.
Nor his wife.
Nor his In laws.
Just Ketan.

I wrote a tweet recently that said, 'don't associate with people
who shit on billionaires. These are people who are more focused
on others than their own lives.'

I know people who despise billionaires.
That can't be me.

I respect anyone who takes a bet on themselves and tries to obtain their version of freedom.
Tons of people will never have the guts to take that bet.
They will just resent from the side.

DON'T FIX WHAT'S NOT BROKEN

The first book series I willingly read was Harry Potter.
It was the first time I was not forced into reading.

My teacher had the first book, Sorcerer's Stone, lying around her class.
It got my curiosity.
I went through a few pages.

And asked her if I could borrow it.
She said yes.

That's what started the Harry Potter journey.

For the next couple of years, I would be on the lookout for when a new book was released.
One by one, I went through each one and enjoyed it.

When the movie series came out, I became a bigger fan.
Started buying Harry Potter shirts.
And once dressed up as Harry for Halloween.

Needless to say, I was getting roasted for acting like this.

Most kids around my age considered Harry Potter to be corny.
They thought me being interested in the series was whack.

I once had a cousin from London visit me.
And him and my brother would roast me as well.
One guy they would constantly make fun of was Dumbledore.

Dumbledore was one of the main characters who served as Harry's mentor.
But as the series progressed, Dumbledore and Harry became friends.

My cousin would call him 'Dumb Old Dork.'

That used to make me irritated.
Especially considering how he was Harry's friend.

As I grew up, I strayed away from Harry Potter.
Still enjoyed the books.
But was no longer a rabid fan like my child self.

I forgot which year it was...
But one day, JK Rowling, the creator of the Harry Potter series
made an announcement.

She said the character Dumbledore, was gay.
Not sure if her readers picked up on it.
However, that was her intention.

When she made that announcement, it automatically sent a lot of
the readers down memory lane.

Wait a minute, really? No way!

Nothing against someone's sexuality.
That's not the point.

The point was how she threw this curveball out of nowhere.
And what was crazier were the 2 groups that formed.

One group was like:

'No way! I guess I'm going to re-read the Harry Potter series and
see what she means.'

Some were like 'Yea, I could see that.'

This group was accepting of Dumbledore being gay.

For the other group, they were like:

'Yea right. You know JK Rowling. She's a great writer. But a
strange person. She's just saying stuff for attention!'

Others would say 'Well, what the hell does she know!'

Just imagine.
People questioning how well the CREATOR of Harry Potter knew
her characters.

At that point....
'Wait a minute!'
What?
'You didn't say which group you were a part of.'
'Uh...'
'Well Armani, which group were you a part of?'
'Okay. I was a part of group 2.'

When she made that announcement, I automatically rejected it.
It's something that didn't register with me.

I thought she was being silly.
Mainly because it did nothing to bring the plot forward in any of
the books.
Just felt like unnecessary detail.

Younger Armani made that conclusion immediately.
It was not something even pondered upon.

Older me doesn't really care.
She is the creator of the book series.
And ultimately, it is her character.

'Any idea why you acted that way as a child? I know you said the
decision was made quick. But any reason you think why that was
the case?'
Yea.

*I felt as though she was trying to fix something that wasn't
broken.*

That happens often in the world of creativity.
Trying to fix something.

Sometimes, the fixing leads to new insights.
A new way of doing things.
A new way of seeing things.

Other times, the fixing is a flop.
It just doesn't register.

One of the Pixar's animators realized how the movie she helped create was now more than a movie.

This particular Pixar creator, let's call her Sally.
Sally helped create Toy Story.

From her end, she saw voiceovers, animation, and movie budgets.
The characters from Toy Story were just that.
Characters.

But her perception towards the characters changed when she saw a father buying his son a Woody action figure.
And the kid started crying.

For the kid, Woody was not just a character.
He was a friend.

Nowadays, I am able to be much more objective with JK Rowling's announcement.

Because nowadays, I am not a hardcore fan.
My emotions aren't so involved in the Harry Potter world.
I see Dumbledore as a character.

But when I was a kid, I was more subjective.
My emotions were involved in the Harry Potter world.
I saw Dumbledore as a friend.

That's why I think the announcement was quickly rejected.

It's because I had to revaluate too many child hood memories.
And then I would have to wait for JK Rowling's message on the other characters as well.

Let me guess, Ron was lowkey a muggle who drank a potion that gave him the power of a wizard?
Well, JK??

That's power I didn't want to give back to the author.
Despite her being the creator.

These sort of psychological insights are unique and show how much impact a story can have on a deep persuasion level.

Rather than reading psychology books all day.
Look at the mirror.

And see how your favorite story impacts you on a psychological and physiological level.

This is a real world class in the world of persuasion.
A look into creating a new world.
And placing people in it.

Storytelling has always been a form of hypnosis.
And for this form of hypnosis, it can be done with words.
No creepy man who is swinging a watch at your face, needed.

DOING THE IMPOSSIBLE

There are 2 types of 'impossible' out there:

1. It's actually impossible.
2 It's perceived as impossible.

I recall when I was 15, I went to this uncle and auntie's house for a party.

The kid in the house was 3 years older than me.

A nerdy looking guy..

We talked for a bit.

He would barely make eye contact with me.

He was too busy looking at his computer.

After some time, he said:

'Yo, my bad man. I made this computer recently, and I need to upgrade the software asap.'

He said that so causally.

'You made that computer?? Yea right!' I said.

He looked back at me puzzled:

'Yea, I made the computer. Why, you don't believe me?'

I said:

'That's impossible! You're barely older than me. You didn't make that!'

That's when he said:

'Take apart all the parts and I'll remake it. If you don't believe me, then buy me new parts and I'll make one for you. I could use some practice.'

When he said that, I believed him.

During that time, if you pressed me, I would have said that it was *possible* to make a computer.

However, I made a rash emotional decision to say it was impossible.

I was projecting my limitations on the other person.

It was not malicious.

It just happened on autopilot.

What my younger self really meant was:

'It's impossible...**for me.**'

The last 2 words are the most important.

I had someone make a comment like that 2+ years ago when I published Level Up Mentality.

A few of my friends bought it.

One of them had it on a bookstand.

We all went to his house one day.

One of the house guests was observing the different books on the stand.

Then he picks up Level Up Mentality, looks at the back, comes up to me...and was like:

'Yo, the guy on the back of this book looks just like you!'

I said, 'that's because it is me.'

Then he looked at me.

'You wrote a book? Yea right! That's impossible.'

Mentally, I finished the sentence for him.

'Yea right!! That's impossible...**for me**.'

Before ruling off something as impossible, add the 'for me' at the end.

There is embarrassment involved.

The brain doesn't like to feel embarrassed because it feels pain.

That's when another narrative is created (hopefully), which is:

'If he or she can do it, then why can't I?'

The question above is what sparks a lot of Level Up journeys.

Resentment, jealousy & self doubt.

Those type of emotions are best channeled towards a higher purpose rather than accepted as a life sentence.

A lot of Level Up journeys start off with competing with others.

But true progress doesn't happen until the participant begins competing with their prior day self.

That's when impossible becomes possible.

FINITE GOALS VS INFINITE GOALS

Infinite goals can be expressed in finite terms.
But finite goals cannot be expressed in infinite terms.

Do you feel like you've stagnated?
Losing motivation?
Finding it difficult to work?

If so, then ambition is low.
Without ambition, work feels like work.
With ambition, work feels like play.

To unleash ambition, reframe finite goals into infinite terms.
'Hm... not sure if I understand what that means?'
Kill deadlines.

Deadlines are great secondary.
But leading with deadlines can lead to sadness.

You ever heard of Ted Turner?
'Yes, the entrepreneur, right?'
Yep.

His dad committed suicide despite being a successful businessman.
It's because his dad felt like he achieved all his goals and had nothing else to live for.

Before he killed himself, he told Ted:

'Set your goals so big that you have no clue if you'd ever achieve them.'

In 2000s, Ted Turner was synonymous with a successful & wealthy entrepreneur.

In order to set infinite goals, strategically use infinite words.

2 being:

-Flawless & forever.

Then apply those words on any skillset that you want to master.

So rather than saying how many blogs you plan to write for the year first..

Say:

'I will become a *flawless* writer.'

'I will skyrocket my writing skills....*forever*.'

Now you have centered yourself on the infinite perspective.

This not only engages the brain, but allows the emotions to spike up.

Emotional Intelligence for Dummies:

-You don't try to fight against your emotions, you learn to work with it.

Fighting against your emotions is like swimming against a tsunami.

Infinite goals engage emotions.

Once you feel empowered, you can reverse engineer the finite goals.

-I plan to write 3 blogs a week.

-Each blog takes roughly 1.5 hours.

-Therefore, I will dedicate 4.5 hours of writing a week.

Then you can reverse engineer how much you want the blog to generate in traffic.

And what you plan to sell to the traffic you attract.

All the numbers come later.

Start off with the infinite goal and build everything around that.

PS:

You don't have to tell others what you are doing.

If you tell others:

'Yea, I'm trying to become a flawless writer.'

They'll laugh at you.

It's because they won't get it.

It's smart to keep infinite goals private.

Having 1 secret with yourself is what builds enthusiasm.

Enthusiasm is an empowering energy built from knowing something that others don't.

So, keep infinite goals private.

Leverage 'flawless' and 'forever' to set an infinite goal.

Build finite goals around that.

And make effort feel effortless.

These are some of the practical insights I drop in my book: *Level Up Mentality: A Guide to Re-Engineer your Mindset for Confidence*

What makes this book different from other mindset books is that it's practical & has an emotional appeal to it as well.

I've had a few people message me and tell me they started crying in chapter 1.

When your emotions get involved, the mind has not option but to listen!

WORKING WITH YOUR HANDS

In 2022, if a kid wants to make more money, the general response is:

-Start an ecom shop

In 2008, if a kid wanted to make more money, the general response was:

-Apply to McDonalds

I spent my late teens working in the Brown People Trifecta:
Subway, Dunkin Donuts, and 7/11

I call these the Brown People Trifecta because these 3 establishments are normally owned by brown people.

My 3 mangers were:
Atul, Ashish and Art
2 Indians and 1 Bengali.

After working for these fellows, I made a conclusion.
-You'll hate working for brown managers.
-You'll love being served by brown managers.

I hated working for these 3 assholes.
They were tyrants.

Wouldn't give breaks.
Would micromanage.
They'd even spy on you!!

In their world view, the customer was ALWAYS right.

I was a teenager at the time.
So I wanted an easy job where I just showed up.

These 3 assholes wanted me to memorize the menu, create small talk with the customers and even tolerate disrespect.
I once had a Biker call me a 'pussy' because I asked him if he wanted cream in his coffee.

These 3 were annoying.
However, they were teaching me a lesson that would take years to internalize.

The lesson of working with your hands.

A person who has had **at least** 1 stage of working with their hands is more battletested.
They are tougher and can deal with pressure.

My experience with the Brown Trifecta came in clutch for my engineering career.
I recall how petty a lot of 'grownups' were.

Most <u>team meetings</u> were code for <u>who can whine the most.</u>
Often, these adults suffered from a pride issue.

Those who worked for Desi managers learned the art of taming their pride.
Which is a crucial skillset.

I've heard the quote:
When your idols become your rivals.

My remix to that quote is:
When those you despised become those you admire.

Nowadays, I don't work in fast-food.
Instead, I'm a customer.
I often get served by the Desi managers I once despised.

When I go to an establishment, I can tell which manager runs
their organization like a well oiled machine...
And who doesn't.

I went to a KFC recently, and the line was long.
Trash wasn't taken out.
And the workers were rude as hell.

One of the workers started to yell at the customer!
I was standing behind the customer who was getting yelled at....

The customer did nothing wrong.
It was the worker who was rude & doing a sloppy job.

I hear the platitude:
'Always judge people based off how they treat the service.'

Yes, the quote is true to a certain extent.
But it can also present an incomplete narrative.

If the customer in front of me who got yelled at...snapped back at the sloppy worker, I wouldn't have judged them at all.

I wouldn't say they should do it. However, I can understand the human side of their response.

I now see why the Desi managers were so strict,.

It's because customers may not always be right.

But if you work in the fast food industry, it's best to operate with the philosophy that the customers are always right.

You will win in the long run.

(This mantra may not be effective in other industries tho).

It's easy to tell who has worked with their hands and who hasn't.

Working with the hands isn't always meant to be taken in a literal sense.

It's more so meant in a symbolic sense.

It's code for:

Do you have any activity that humbles you?

When I worked in 7/11, I had to roll these heavy ass carpets, pick it up and shake it outside to remove the dirt.

People walked on these carpets with their dirty shoes.

And here I was, rubbing it on my shirt as I took it outdoors.

All for 7.25$ per hour?

That was a task that hurt my pride during the time.

But after, it built thick skin.

Modern generations may have felt sorry for me.

'Damn man, you really had to do those physical jobs? That sucks!'

No, my friend.

It didn't suck.

Heck, it was a crash course on soft skills.

Only when you control your pride is when you unlock a deeper understanding of thick skin, maturity and consistency.

When you're judging a position because you feel sorry for them...

See how they are working.

They maybe getting a crash course on something that will benefit them in the future.

BEING A PROFESSIONAL

Have you ever wondered what being 'a professional' was?
What's the first thing that comes to your mind?

'Um...someone who is wearing a suit and tie!'
Eh, we can do better.

That's the outer appearance
It's much deeper than that.

'What's your definition of someone who is a professional?'
I consider someone a professional when I can't tell their emotional state based on their work.

'Huh???'
Let me give you an example.

Let's say you're a woman named Susie.
You have been waiting to get your hair done for a few weeks now.

The day you go to the salon...
Michelle, your stylist, has a mopey face.
She looks visibly upset.

For the next hour, she goes to work on your hair.
Your back is facing the mirror.
So you can't see how she is doing.

After 1.5 hours, she turns you around.

There it is.....

ONE OF THE WORST HAIRCUTS YOU HAVE EVER SEEN IN YOUR LIFE.

Normally, Michelle is so great with your hair.

What happened today?

You let her know that you're disappointed and ask her what happened?

Then she responds with:

'I'm so sorry.. My puppy died this morning & I am just out of it.'

Now, 2 sides of Susie kicks in.

1.

Susie understands why Michelle fucked up her hair.

Susie has a dog & can't imagine working after losing her beloved pet.

2.

The other side of Susie kicks in.

She is a bridesmaid at her sister's wedding. That's why she was getting her hair done in the first place.

How embarrassing is it going to be for Susie as she walks in the wedding looking like a straight up clown?

Now let's ask....

Was the hair stylist a professional or not?

If you were to ask me, the answer is no.
She was **not** a professional.

With my definition of a professional, I do not want to REMOTELY know if you're having a good day or a bad day based on your work.
Work, then process your feelings in outside zones.

Ironically, you can use work to process your feelings better!
Those with the highest EQ use their work to take their internal world to the gym.

This is where the field of emotional intelligence often gets misinterpreted by the public.

When someone thinks of 'emotional intelligence' they may picture someone crying in a corner or crying in group.
It may imply 'getting in touch with your feelings.'

Getting in touch with your feelings is not meant to be something soft.
Instead, it's supposed to be internal technology that allows us to rise when life is going well *or* not going well.

'Should I judge people for not being a professional?'
Nah...

There are a few more variables to consider.
1. Some people hate their jobs and will never be a professional.

2. Others are temporarily going to be out of their game because the trauma is that strong.

Therefore, labeling someone as a professional should be a RARE occurrence.

A true professional deserves the utmost respect.

Problems are not a bug in mother nature.

Problems are a feature of mother nature.

These consistent people who always show up & don't make their emotional state known (especially the bad) also have their fair share of problems.

They are probably sick, lost pets, loved ones, have stress etc.

However, they still show up.

By the way...

Any bubba can physically show up.

Only a **few** can show up with a limitless attitude.

When they bring their body to work, they bring their mind too.

Being a professional in your industry is deeper than just dressing in formal clothes...

It's a character trait.

A trait that gifts you admission to the 3% club.

MAKE WRITING FUN AGAIN

I met this one writer a few years ago at a networking event.
He was the first ever author I met..

As we talked, he mentioned how he wrote 2 books in 14 years.

When I first heard that, I thought:
'Damn, 2 books in 14 years. That's all?'

I probably shouldn't have thought that.
Oh well....

As we talked more, he shared his writing process with me.
He talked about how he wrote a few sentences, spent the next 30 minutes polishing those sentences up, then he would write the next few sentences.

As he talked about his writing process, I wanted to jump of a building!
His process sounded like torture.

He gave me a repulsed feeling towards writing.
We talked for some time & then I dipped.

A few years later, I realized I judged this guy too soon.
That's **his** writing process.
If it works for him, go for it...

'Do you agree with his process?'

Hell no!

My philosophy is fundamentally different than his.

THE ARMANI WRITING FORMULA:
-Create like no one will see your writing.
-Edit like everyone will see your writing.

The reason I didn't vibe with this writer's process was because he created and edited at the same time.

My formula is against that.

It's important to separate creating and editing because each stage requires completely different hats.

When you create, you want to:
-take risks, be fearless, use emotion.

When you edit, you want to:
-not take risks, be a scaredy cat, use logic.

Trying to create & edit at the same time will make writing feel like a pain in the ass.

Creating THEN editing will make writing feel fun.

I measure my creating success based on how little I use the backspace button when I'm typing.

Just keep moving.

The hard part is the creating part.

VERY FEW people actually create.

What they do is the regurgitate.

They hear other peoples thoughts and opinions & provide opinions on that.

A lot of commentators in this world.

Few creators.

NOBODY KNOWS ANYTHING

According to Henry Ford, there are 2 types of people:

- Those who generate ideas.
- Those who execute on the ideas that have been generated.

If you look around, most of the jobs that are done with bare hands are someone else's idea.

You ask the person who thought of the idea:

'How did you think of the idea?'

They will give a vague response.

Some will give a scientific response.

They will use logic to reverse engineer how they got the idea.

But if you pressed them even further, they'll say that there was a level of inspiration that guided them to the scientific analysis in the first place.

When filmmakers are often asked:

'How do you get the ideas for your movies?'

They are like:

'Hm... I'm not sure.'

That sounds like a strange response!

How are you able to create a concrete thing like a movie from a blurry concept like 'Hm...I'm not sure' ???

Here is one group of people doing very **real** acts with their hands and their mind.

But the person who created those ideas in the first place is talking about ambiguous topics like inspiration.

What gives?

The bottom line is that no one knows anything.

They are figuring it out through a systematic process.

Once they learn it, they share it.

What worked 10 years ago does not always mean it will work now.

'Are there any principals which stay the same?'

Of course.

Most of the topics that this newsletter covers were relevant 1000 years ago and will be relevant 1000 years from now.

Speaking, writing, building concentration skills etc.

These are primal skills.

But how they are USED may be different from era to era.

Let's talk about the big homie, Aristotle.

He was known as a great public speaker.

But want to know something?

'What?'

He didn't have the tools to *watch* his speech back.

He'd often rely on feedback from this audience.

The concept of watching his speech back was an idea that didn't even exist for him!

He'd consider it magic or witchcraft.

For our era, watching your speech back is 100% doable.

You get a camera and record your talk.

It can all be done with a click of a button!

The public speaking is the same.

But there is a remix.

When someone says:

'No one knows anything.'

That is a translation for:

'Just because something worked then doesn't mean it will work now.'

And:

Just because something didn't work then doesn't mean it will not work now.'

This is a great perspective because it leads to a mindset known as:

- **Open minded skepticism.**

Humans often undermine how biased they are.

Humans often undermine how biased others are.

They aren't biased for malicious reasons.

They can be biased due to:

- Lack of information.
- Identifying strongly with an experience at the expense of other experiences.
- Inability to focus for long periods of time.

It's best for a pioneer to listen to all.

But over time, cultivate a baseline set of principles that allow them to evaluate what works and doesn't work for their life.

Only then will the pioneer understand the ambiguous phrases like inspiration, that led to a solid decision.

COACHING VS CONSULTING

There's a big difference between coaching and consulting.

It's wise to know the difference even if you don't have a service based business.

Coaching is interactive.

A coach holds you accountable, gives you a game plan, and gives necessary encouragement.

Consulting is a bit less interactive.

The consultant will often do the work for you or tell you what to do.

'Which one is better?'

It's not about comparing them.

It's about knowing when to apply which.

For an out of shape person...

They will probably need a coach.

Where they have someone holding them accountable, telling them what to improve, and keeping them pushing forward.

While someone who want tips on website development will hire a consultant to get the new website changes made.

Imagine flipping the 2.

Imagine giving a consultant to a guy who needs to get in shape.

The guy who needs to get in shape is given a diet plan and a workout plan.

But isn't given motivation to keep on going.

And a guy who wants his website changed is given a coach.
'Come on!! You can do this. Click update! You can do it!!'

Sure, even in the alternate satiations, solutions can be reached.
But the process will be suboptimal.

Just knowing the difference between consulting a coaching is
a **significant** advantage.
Now it's just a matter of reading people and seeing what path
they need.

*And PS: Often, people have no clue what path they REALLY
need.*

SHARED EXCITEMENT

Around 2017, there was this random phone number that called me.

I answered.

It was a lady who asked:

'Hello, is this Arman Chowdhury?

I said, *yes, it is*.

She began giving me a sales pitch.

She was like:

'Mr. Chowdhury. We discovered you through Instagram. We believe you will be a great test class for our new app.'

I asked her what the app was about.

She said it was for matchmaking.

It was an app that was going to get brown people like me and assign them a matchmaker.

The matchmaker would coordinate calls in order to set up a relationship.

I had just gotten out of a relationship and didn't want to jump into another one.

So, I told the lady *no thanks*.

She was like:

'Mr. Chowdhury. Did I mention it will be free?'

Free? you say.

Okay, what the hell...

Go on and sign me up.

So, she got my info and created me a profile.

She needed me to confirm some stuff the following week.

But I never did.

A few years goes on by.

In 2019, she hits me up again.

She's like:

'Mr. Chowdhury, I've been looking for you for so long. How come you haven't been answering my calls??'

I had been getting so many spam calls, that I rarely pick up a number if I don't recognize it.

I apologized and asked her why she was contacting me.

She was like:

'Mr. Chowdhury, you have a few of matches. But there is 1 particular woman who would really like to meet you. Can you please do the call?'

I saw her profile.

She was from Texas.

I thought about it...

Eh, sure why not?

So, I got on a call with the girl.

Let's call her Mila.

Mila seemed like a cool person.

She was the sister of one of my fraternity brothers from New Jersey.

She seemed to have a good head on her shoulders.

Until....

Somewhere in the convo, Mila informed me that this match making app was **very popular**.

Apparently, she was paying roughly 100 dollars a month for it!

I was like:

'You're paying that much??'

She was like:

'Yea. How much are you paying?'

My matchmaker never asked me for credit card info.

It was because I was one of the initial participants to be asked.

Since I was a test group, my payment was waived.

I told her I wasn't paying anything.

Then I shared the story of how I was bought into the app.

How they asked me to sign up after finding my Instagram.

I told the story as a joke.

But I didn't get any laughs.

When I told her that, the entire tone of the convo was off.

This Mila chick became very cold.

She was like:
'What? Everyone else is paying, that's not fair.'

This Mila girl was bringing it up in a way where she was like:
'We should even get the initial participants to pay a fee!'

The more I talked to Mila, the more she repulsed me.
This is a chick that I want nowhere near me.
This was the behavior of someone who gave me snake vibes.

I learned something from that conversation:
-People **hate** things to be unfair.

Had the situation been flipped, I don't think the whole ordeal would have been a big deal at all.
I would have gotten a laugh that Mila was getting it for free, and I was paying 100.

But who knows?
I wasn't in the circumstance.

Anyways, an easy way to be likable in situations like this is to share enthusiasm when someone has something that you don't.
Which is difficult to do.

The body **hates** when things are unfair.
It feels physical pain.
But take yourself out of it and see the situation from their lens.

That view point will build relationships.

And lack of that viewpoint will cause the destruction of potential relationships.

SOFTENING UP MISTAKES

This is a quick message for today.

I wanted to break down a tweet that I wrote yesterday.

The tweet was:

People are forgiving when you give them updates

So if you do miss a deadline, they aren't shocked with the information

When you give unpleasant surprises like that... it makes you look bad & enrages them

Soften up errors with updates

There is a psychological insight that I want to share.

Let's say your name is Ramon & you own a construction company.

You are working with this newly wed couple to add a new room to their house.

They are ecstatic for this new room because they are expecting a child.

Your project was going smooth in the initial stages.

However, mid way in, 1 of your employees decides to quit.

The other one caught COVID and is out for a few weeks.

This suddenly ruins the initial deadline you were expecting.

It's easy to avoid giving an update to them.

'If I tell them I'll be late, then they will get mad.'

But you being late is inevitable.

Might as well give updates & give them in volume!

Because when Ramon is giving those updates, he creates a:

'We are in this together' mentality.

He starts to create a bond with the newly wed couple.

When the bond is being cultivated, a friendship is being formed.

A person is much less likely to yell at someone they consider a friend.

It's better to create updates with sprinkles of hope rather than hitting them with a TSUNAMI of bad news at once.

This was my quick message for today.

I don't know how you will use it.

Maybe you're running late in a consulting project.

Or maybe you hired a coach & you've been slacking with the assignments he gave you.

Stay in front of their mind with explanations.

Good or bad, they are much more likely to view you as a friend.

DARK SIDE OF MASTERY

A little bit embarrassing to say.
But here it goes...

A few years ago, I was a big fan of professional eating.
Was fascinated with how the sport worked.

'Did you just call eating a sport??'
Yea, I did.

I didn't know it was a sport.
Thought eating was just eating.
However, there was a short, ripped Asian man who changed my perspective.

His name was Takeru Kobayashi.

I initially saw Takeru on this MTV documentary.
There was a short clip of him flexing his abs.
The documentary was exploring the world of professional eating.

Takeru looked like an audience member who came to watch the professional eaters eat.
But no...
He was a participant.

How??

I thought professional eaters were these fat dudes who were eating hotdogs.
How the hell are you that low in body fat percentage, despite eating that much?
His abs looked like they were painted on.

I started to hear more about Takeru Kobayashi after that documentary.
Every 4th of July, there is a hot dog eating competition in Coney Island.

There was a year when Takeru SHATTERED the pre-existing records.
He put the world on notice...

He intrigued me because I was a skinny wimpy kid at the time.
Before my 11 inch growth spurt, I was 5'2.
Thought I was going to be short for the rest of my life.

Takeru wasn't that tall. He was 5'8.
He gave me inspiration to get the block 6 pack like him.
However, I was more intrigued about the fast eating.
Could I do it too?

Around the time, my parents would buy food for me and my brother.
We'd often get burritos & hot dogs as snacks at home.

I told my brother he could have all the burritos if I could have all the hot dogs.
He reluctantly agreed.

For the next few days, I practiced eating hot dogs very fast.
I wanted to be like Takeru...

At first, I was eating it one bite at a time.
Just like how regular people eat it.

Later on, after doing some research, I realized I was doing it wrong.
I was supposed to be preparing for the next bite, while on the first bite.

That way, I become faster, and create more of a flow.
Staying 1 step ahead of the game.

I also learned a dry mouth was destructive.
Gotta stay hydrated!
The more hydrated you are, the less resistance you face with the hot dogs.

Another thing I learned was that you should stretch your mouth, so you can take bigger bites.

The more I practiced, the more I learned.
Takeru was the north star that I was learning from him.

'How old were you when you got curious about professional eating?'
I was 15 at the time.

After spending MONTHS on eating fast, I started to find other interests.
I liked professional eating.
However, I wasn't planning on making a career out of it or anything.

I came back to reality & started to do what normal kids would do.
Enrolled in karate & forgot about my venture with eating fast.

FAST FORWARD

3 years ago, I was eating with a few coworkers.
We would often go off campus on Fridays.

On this particular Friday, we decided to go to Costco's.
Costco's has some amazing hotdogs which could fill you up for the entire day.

Soon as we sat and started eating....
Old school Armani kicked in.

It's like the muscle memory of eating hot dogs fast was still there.
I had the flexibility in my mouth to finish those large hotdogs in under a minute.

My coworkers looked at me and were like:
What the fuck? Are you done already??'

I proudly nodded my head.
I thought they were going to give me some praise.

Instead, they began making fun of me.
'Damn boi, you're a fatass! Hahaha.'

They didn't understand the technique I knew.

Their mind couldn't process how I once spent hours researching, applying, failing, fine tuning to achieve this fast pace.

I spent so many hours on eating fast that I wasn't trying to impress anyone at Costco's.
A conscious act simply became a subconscious one.

I by no means am a master in professional eating.
I don't think I'd even qualify for a local competition.

But what I do know is that mastery comes with darkness.
'What's the darkness?'
How you make the difficult look easy.

It's like when a fat man looks at the boxer who is risking his life getting hit on the head & says:
'If I were the boxer, I'd stop being such a pussy & throw more jabs.'

It's like when an entitled person who never turned 1$ into 2$ says:
'Those damn billionaires are the reason that I'm broke & live such a sad life. Wish I was privileged like them.

It's like when that guy who has never created anything says:
'Let me steal from this prolific creator. He already has plenty of ideas. I deserve some of those ideas.'

-Fantasy: The masses admire mastery.

-Reality: Pockets of people admire mastery, while the masses are completely ignorant of mastery or downright ridicule it.

This is how it is.
This is why you should never work for praise.

If you get the praise, it will rarely be what you expected.
It'll be a quick 'good job.'
Then the person will go back to their lives.

Other times, you are making the difficult look so seamless, that they won't see anything praiseworthy in the first place.

And other times, these people you seek praise from will outright
ridicule you & make it seem like you didn't work for everything
that you have.

Be self motivated.
Have a burning desire to improve.
Don't need praise from **anyone**.

What are you currently trying to improve?
And are you doing it for the right reasons?
Or are you just trying to get those few temporarily pats on the
back?

This newsletter covers communication skills.
When you think communication, you may immediately think
'external.'

However, the subject which deals the most with the 'external' has
a funny way of leading us back to the 'internal.'

Do it for yourself first.
Give yourself a pat on the back.
That's how you take a giant leap towards mastery.

CAN'T IMPRESS EVERYONE

A few days ago, I released a video called how to build a stronger voice.
For the most part, it added clarity for others.

Got some emails saying that it was an eye opener on the voice.
It helped the viewers understand that the voice is not like height.
It's malleable.

Not everyone was impressed though.
I got a comment saying:
'Really this needs to be taught.'

Something like that.

Initially, I misread the comment.
I thought it was written like:
'Really, this needs to be taught!!"

I thought the comment was showing enthusiasm.
I responded back with, 'Yep, it's a skillset.'

Next morning, I get a comment back from the person who wrote:
'I wasn't agreeing with you, I was LMAO.'
They went onto say that the topic of building a stronger voice
didn't need to be taught.

I looked at the handle.
It was a woman.

Initially, the video was meant for men.
I'm sure some women would like to strengthen their voice too.

The tips in the video can be applied to all genders.
However, I noticed that I normally get questions on how to build
a more resonant voice from guys.

More specifically, guys with low confidence.

Yes, this lady doesn't know the background of an unconfident guy.
She can't perceive the experience.

Let's say a guy has an ugly face.
Is short.
Broke.
Doesn't have any skillsets.

Sure, the skillsets & the money can be worked on.
Even fashion can be improved.

The more variables that can be adjusted, the more **potential** for confidence this guy sees.

Having a resonant voice for a group of men has always been intriguing.
A fragile voice is a silent worry they face (pun intended).

When a guy has a voice that breaks in public, he may view himself to be weak.
Doubt permeates the mind.

I'm not remotely upset by the way..
I wanted to tell the story of this angry lady because this leads me to the real story for today...

There's this one gym trainer that I followed over a decade ago.
His content was mainly to help skinny guys gain muscle.

I noticed he was very specific with his niche.
He even called himself Skinny Vinny.

I saw myself in Skinny Vinny.
Enjoyed the narrative.
One of the first fitness YouTubers I recall watching.

He wasn't trying to help everyone.
He was trying to help skinny guys gain their first 30 pounds of muscle.

That was the blueprint that started off his career.
My high school self resonated with him a lot.

Over a decade later, I came to notice a stunning parallel.
Where Skinny Vinny helped a lot of skinny guys....
Thus far, the ArmaniTalks brand has helped a lot of shy guys.

I thought it was an interesting connection.
I looked to see what Skinny Vinny was up to nowadays.

Noticed he was getting more criticism on his channel and
downvotes.
Hmm..why?

That's when I saw that he changed the focus of his channel.
He was no longer centered around being solely a fitness brand.
Instead, he was now a brand that helped fitness people build
businesses.

Why the backlash? I wondered.

I don't exactly know why.
But what I do know is that you can't impress everyone.

I'm sure there were a lot of guys like me he attracted with his
videos from 10 years back.
Those people **expected** fitness content from him.

When he was transitioning to 'business content' I think they
viewed him as 'selling out.'
That's why there was resistance to his sudden shift in focus.

Not everyone left.
Plenty subscribers stood by him...
Watching his videos to this day.
I plan to be one of those individuals.

I like it when a person is evolving over time.
Expecting someone to be the same for life is idiotic.

I'm sure the people who switched up are not a creator in any
facet of life.
They consume a lot.
But they don't understand the creation process.

'What should I know about the creation process?'
You should know that creation and consumption go hand in hand.

A person who outputs also inputs.

As Skinny Vinny transitioned from the 28 year old fitness youtuber to the 41 year old business/fitness youtuber, he changed along the way.

He inputted new information.
Got married.
Had 3 kids.

Expecting him to be the same 28 year old person is asinine and not right.

I don't know much about him nowadays.
Completely got lost from his work for over 10 years.
Maybe he did people wrong. I have no clue.

I'm writing this post with the assumption that others turned on him for changing the theme of his brand.

My philosophy is to focus on the micro over macro when it comes to people.
Numbers give the false illusion of success.
Making it seem like all these people are your fiends.

They can't all be your friends, bud.
Never could.
Never will.

Some will stick by you through the up's and down's.
Those are the real ones.

The lady who was critical of my video would never understand how a shy guy making his voice just a TAD bit deeper can make him feel 2 inches taller.

I could logically break it down.
However, she just wouldn't get it.

So, I dropped a heart on her comment & went about my day.
As I recommend you do as well when someone just doesn't get it
with you.

Only a few people are meant to 'get it.'
They resonate with you.
It's because you are serving as a a Skinny Vinny in their world.

WHY I DO WHAT I DO

The concept of impromptu speaking is an uncharted territory from my point of view.
The concept of impromptu writing is even more uncharted.

Something about impromptu always has spoke to me.
It gives me strong feelings within.
Which is the feelings someone feels when they find something that is **right** for them.

I didn't get why earlier.
Nowadays, I still don't get why I get those feelings.

However, I have different ideas that my younger self couldn't articulate.

It comes down to uncertainty.
The power of probability distributions.

At the quantum level, Newtonian laws begin to break down.
'English please!'
The rules that work for macro does not work with micro.

The world around us is solid.
That's the domain that can be perceived by the mind.

However, in the micro world, things seem different.
At a spooky level.

That's when a particle based reality is replaced for a probabilistic one.
A probabilistic reality is **only** possible when uncertainty is involved.

'Why are you saying all this again?'
It's because I started to notice a parallel between physics and communication.

Newtonian communication = Planning
Quantum communication = Impromptu

I see a ton of value in planning & getting your notes ready.
Heck, that's what most individuals should look at.

However, I am very cognizant of a hidden fear that some have.

I have a section in my website where I offer a free 15 minute consultation.
It's an application process where some people are chosen.

The hidden pain I notice is the fear of being called on when they are not EXPECTING it.

Maybe it's when they are at a work meeting.
Suddenly, the leader of the meeting looks at Jacob and asks 'Can you break down the root cause of the P1 from last week?'

This creates panic.
A skipped heartbeat.
A tense forehead.
Elbows tighten up.

'How are you able to get so specific with what they feel?'
Because they tell me.

These moments of panic create a snapshot in the memory bank.
It's a fear.

Another situation is when a businessman is on the phone with a difficult client.
And the client asks a question that stumps this businessman.

That fear of being judged for being stuck & not being able to do anything about it, causes a different set of physical sensations in this businessman..

Nevertheless, strong physical sensations indicating discomfort are created.

The point is that nothing is fully certain in nature.
I never said 'stop planning what you are going to say.'
Planned talks are magic.

But unplanned talks are mystical.

There's something phenomenal about creating during moments
of uncertainty.
When you go from a Newtonian being into a Quantum one.

That's when ideas that NO ONE else is sharing...
Is being shared.

The world of Newtonian is the comfort zone.
If a person is trying to escape the comfort zone in every facet of
life, then it'll be a hassle.

You probably don't hear that too often.
It's easy to say 'always escape the comfort zone!'

Not quite.
Some things are better with boundaries.

I'm happy that drivers on the highway are in the comfort zone.
The last thing I want is a daredevil on the road.
Trying to take risks.
Follow the rules buddy, so we all get home safely.

However, there are certain parts of life where the comfort zone
needs to be shattered.
When uncertainty needs to be experienced.

I do what I do with impromptu speaking & impromptu
writing because I think this is what was meant to be produced on
the internet.

Not cookie cutter viewpoints on things.
Instead, allow different worlds to merge.

Only in this newsletter will you see communication and physics
merging.
It's because the worlds seem different.
Yet, they are very similar.

When working with physical rulesets, everything looks different.
When working with knowledge rulesets, everything becomes
identical.

SERVANT AND THE MASTER

The phrase "servant" can be seen in different contexts based on
the person hearing it.

If you're a Western reader, this word may leave a sour taste in
your mouth.
Sure, servants exist.
But something about it seems wrong.

On the other hand, if you're an Eastern reader, then it's different.
Servants are normal.

When I was living in Bangladesh as a little kid, I used to be cool
with my servants.
One of the guy's name was Bilal.

I was 4 ish at the time.
Bilal looked like he was in his mid 20s.
Maybe even younger.

He was a friend to me and my brother.
We actually had no clue that he 'worked' for the family.

**In plenty of countries overseas, a servant and a master
have a synergistic relationship.**

A master may seem threatening to a Western mind.
On the contrary, in the households with servants, a master is seen
as a protector.

'Why do you say a synergistic relationship is created?'
Because the servant needs a place to stay and food to eat.

A lot of them lived in the streets beforehand.
Homelessness is a norm in several 3rd world countries.

So when they are chosen for a household, a part of them thinks
they won the lottery.

But remember this bucko...

No such thing as a free lunch.
You need to hustle.

This servant is given clothes, food, and friendship.
In return, they must *work*.

They must prepare the meals for the household.
Do the daily tasks, like laundry and all of that.
If there is a rat in the house, then they will have to step up
and 'handle it.'

The point of this email comes down to **perspectives**.
After reading what I wrote so far, some people may be like,
*'Forreal, servants are a norm in certain parts of the world?? No
way!'*

And other people are like,
'Why are you bringing up common sense to me??'

Perspective is the name of the game when dealing with others.
It's more important now than ever.

I had a guy from Honduras a while back working on a small flyer
for me.
I noticed... HE WOULD WRITE IN ALL CAPS OUT OF THE
BLUE MOON!!!

Sometimes, I thought he was yelling at me.
He'd often write in all caps right after I requested he
fix something.

So this seemed like a threatening move to me.
Didn't appreciate it.

Overtime, I noticed he didn't do this in a malicious way.
Heck, after a project, the seller and the buyer can leave each
other a review.
I'd give him a 5 star review.

He'd write in his review:
'THIS CLIENT IS GREAT. THANK YOU FOR TRUSTING ME.'

Hm....

All caps again.
But this time, it is meant in a positive context.

Wait, was it always meant in a positive context?
I believe so.

In the interconnected world we live in, a cross combination of cultures are happening in real time.
-What is considered rude for one party is considered a norm for the other.
-What is considered a norm for one party is seen as blasphemy by the other.

In a land where parties are quick to be outraged.
Be the person who is quick to be curious...

BECUSE YOU MAY JUST LEARN SOMETHING ABOUT SERVANTS AND MASTERS IN THE PROCESS.

DOESN'T HURT TO ASK

In 2019, I was a part of an event in Tampa called 'Be Inspired to Inspire.'
It was an event for local entrepreneurs around the area.

Initially, I wanted to be a speaker.
However, the host of the event said that the speaker positions were out.
She said I could come in as an audience member. I was bummed out, but agreed.

As some time went on by, she asked if I wanted to be an emcee.
I said 'yes, I'd like that.'

That was my first experience as an emcee and I enjoyed it.
It was fun, because you go wide, not deep.
A speaker gives a very nuanced talk on a subject.
The emcee serves as the glue guy.

After the event, a public speaking coach I was working with whispers in my ear, **'get reviews.'**

I asked him, 'of what?'
That's when he slapped me on the head in a gentle manner and was like, 'of what people thought of your emceeing!'

He was a large bald man with a friendly smile. He seemed like what Santa Claus would look like without hair or a beard. A jolly man.

It was hard not to like him.

I thought this was a brilliant idea!
A review never hurts a product or service.

So I start going around the event afterwards asking different people if they could give a 30 second clip of what they thought.
Most people agreed.

However, 1 person said, 'No, I'm good.'

I thought he was the FIRST person who would agree to the review!

Throughout the event, we were the one's coordinating behind the scenes.
In the beginning of the event, he was the one helping me pass things out and make sure things were going smooth.

I thought he was my boy.
Thought he was going to be like, 'Hell yea man. Count me in.'

But he flat out said, 'No, I'm good.'

What was ironic was that people who I thought wouldn't give a review were some of the most enthusiastic in volunteering.

There was a middle aged woman who had just gotten fired from her job.
She had the face of someone who had just gotten fired.
Very serious and rigid with a noticeable frown.

While I was on stage, I'd make eye contact with this lady a few times and would think, 'Damn, she must be having an awful time.'

After the event, I didn't even directly ask her to give her thoughts.
Instead, I asked a person she was accompanied by.
That's when the sour faced woman volunteered herself. 'Hello young man, let me go next!' she said.

How peculiar is that?

People who I thought were going to be eager to volunteer said no and people who I thought weren't going to be eager to volunteer said yes.

I guarantee if you take 5 days, you'll think of a few situations like this yourself!

Which brings me to the ultimate point of this talk:
'It doesn't hurt to ask.'

It's a numbers game.

Not a completely wild gun approach, of course.
Instead, somewhat tactical, but not **too** tactical.

Being too tactical makes someone an overthinker...
Or worse, a coward.

If I was too tactical asking everyone for a review that day, I'd be
judging people by their mean faces.
A lot of them had mean faces.
Some were gentle.
However, the faces weren't always indicating who would say yes
or no.

**The ball is back on your court when you ask and live
with whatever they say.**

There are billions of people on this planet.
If one person says no, then all good, move on to the next.

If I only asked the guy who I thought was going to say yes (but
ended up saying no).... then I would be daydreaming about that
all day.

'Geez, why did he say no to the review?'
'I thought we were friends?'
'Does he like me?'

Blah blah blah.

It was never personal.
More importantly, it was never that serious.
I came to find out from that man's wife that he was camera shy.

Plenty of people who like public speaking hate speaking in front
of a camera.
It gets them terrified.
Not uncomfortable, but **terror** hits.

Yep.
It's rarely personal.
Never hurts to ask.

1. Ask in a way where you assume the person is going to say yes.

2. If they say no, give them the benefit of the doubt as if they were scared.

That 2 step dynamic creates a bold winner through the process of asking questions.

EVOLUTION ON CAMERA

A couple of years ago, I began following this one YouTuber who gave practical strategies on running a YouTube channel.
She talked about seo, how to read the analytics and how to get passive income.

She was a blonde hair blue eyed girl.

In the initial stages, i followed her only for her practical stuff.
I guess this got the algorithm thinking it would be smart to recommend her second channel...which was vlog based.

Eh, not interested.
Nothing against her, but I don't really watch that vlogging stuff.

The algorithm continued to persist.
After the 4 time of being recommended the channel, I decided to subscribe.

I would rarely watch the videos.
Every now and then, I'd see a clip art along with the title.
It looked like she had a boyfriend and they were moving.
Nice.

As more time passed on by, I saw a thumbnail which caught my attention.
It was an image of her crying.

Looking at this clip, I saw that it dwarfed all her other videos in terms of numbers. Clearly, the thumbnail was attention grabbing.
Decided to see what was up.

In the video, she shared how her boyfriend had cheated on her.
To make matter worse, they had gotten married without telling much people.
So not only was she breaking up, she was getting a formal divorce as well.

For the next few months, she documented herself rebuilding. She tried new hobbies, downloaded new dating apps, went hiking and all that.

She was chronicling herself out of darkness.

A few weeks ago, it had been her 1 year anniversary of the breakup video.
In order to celebrate, she was going to create a reaction video to the video from the year earlier.

This was inception.
The girl was watching herself!

You could tell it was tough on her watching herself taking such a massive L.
However, you could also tell the person watching this year was vastly different from the year before.

I wonder what will happen next year? Is she going to watch a video of herself watching the video from the year earlier??
I sense a series…

This was a good look into how communication is evolving in real time. This girl will have a part of her life documented for a long time unless she decides to delete the video or put it on private.

Speaking of private….

Since starting the ArmaniTalks brand, I've gotten a lot of people to check out Toastmasters or start journaling. Some people decided to do both.

It's great getting emails and dms of the people who noticed practical benefits. Those who didn't, all good as well.

One new idea I want to push more is the private YouTube channel. An idea I rarely see being discussed.

A couple of years back, I had gotten a client who was high up in his company. Introverted and wanted to be more expressive. That's when we created a private channel for him to speak.

His impromptu speaking skills improved, idea muscle strengthened and he could articulate much better.

Since that channel, he went onto start a podcast where he interviews industry leaders in a variety of fields.

Just imagine how much value was created in ripple effects? Imagine how many business deals happened after rapport was built in those interview sessions?

The YouTuber who I followed was a public channel. So more props to her for putting herself out like that.

On the other hand, we all need to start somewhere.

Someone may want to use their phone and internet for more than mindlessly scrolling on social media all day..
But have no clue where to get started.

Added to this, they don't feel comfortable articulating their ideas in front of others.

Added even more to this, they find out they can't concentrate for longer than 8 seconds at a time.
That's correct.

Having a conversation is great. But conversations can mask poor concentration skills. It's because you have someone to bounce ideas off. Strictly speaking by yourself is a beast that only a few can conquer.

That's why I want to push the private YouTube channel more. It's sort of like a visual journal when you think about it.

This girl will be happy to keep reviewing how far she came from the year before.

Just like generation wealth is about passing down resources. Generational content is about passing down ideas.

A channel that starts private does not have to remain private. Making it public is all about dragging and dropping from a certain menu.

I'm not going to discuss that, you can Google it.

This is a place that you can see yourself grow up in real time and review back.

When you're 40 years older, you can be like, 'man, I used to record on this YouTube channel, let me see what's up with that.'

Others will record even 40 years later if YouTube doesn't self implode.

Share ideas. Watch ideas back. Evolve ideas.

In this world, some people become the servants to technology. Others decide to become the masters.

THIN SKIN IS THY NAME

It's hard to admit being thin skinned or highly sensitive in the present moment.
Luckily, it's much easier to admit being thin skinned when going down memory lane.

In my late teens and early 20s, I was very thin skinned.
My feelings would get hurt easily.
There is one memory that sticks out...

Tampa has an annual parade known as the Gasparilla parade.
This is when a bunch of residents in Tampa dress up as pirates and check out the floats.
All in good fun.

I didn't like parades when I was 19.

The year prior, I heard some scary news.
Heard there were some crazy people that had needles with some chemicals and they went around poking people in the crowded festival.

Other than that, I'm not one of those guys who likes crowded areas where I'm rubbing elbows with people.

However, I was the only one with a car from my friend circle.
So they all asked me to go.
I mean they forced me.

Being the designated driver was one thing.
But what made the trip irritating was that one of my friend's invited this girl named Ronaq.

She was what I call Ms. Sarcastic.
Some people love sarcasm, some people find it annoying.
I'm the latter.

As soon as she gets in my car, which is packed, she starts talking a lot.

When I slow down at the yellow light, she starts commenting on how I should have sped past it.

Eventually, she asks me a question like, *'can you even drive??'*
This annoying person was getting under my skin.

The breaking point for me came during a talk on cats and dogs.
I had known this vet who told me that cats and dogs use their tails differently.

A dog wags their tail a lot when they are happy.
A cat wags their tail a lot when they are unhappy.

When the conversation of dogs and cats came up, I decided I was going to share the insight that this vet shared with me!
When I shared my insight, I was lowkey hoping to get a pat on the back.

Then this Ronaq girls blurts out, *'Yea right! Dogs and cats both wag their tails when they are happy.'*

It's like she had an opinion for everything...

That's when we reached our destination.
I was in the mood to debate with her and let her know that she was wrong.
However, she seemed eager to get out the car and go to the parade.

As we were in the parade, I tried pulling up articles discussing the difference between the tails of dogs and cats.
However, due to how crowded it was, I couldn't get an internet connection.

This bothered me.
Not just a little.
But a lot.

I **needed** to let Ronaq know that she was wrong and that I was right.
Otherwise, I simply couldn't enjoy this parade.

Still, the slow internet was an issue from the parade to the
restaurant to the after party....

Around late at night, once we were all coming back home, I was
eagerly plotting my comeback.
I already had in mind exactly what I was going to type into
Google to get the answers.
Just wait till we pull over.

Once we all get back to the initial meetup spot getting ready to
wave our goodbyes, I search away on Google.

Before the people disperse, I'm like, *'Ronaq wait!'*
She turns around.

That's when I hand her my cellphone in a confident way with an
article and told her to read it.
It was an article talking about how dogs and cats move their tails
differently.

As she read it with curiosity, she eventually hands the phone back
to me and was like, *'Are you still thinking about that??? You're
such a girl!'*

That's when she makes everyone aware of how I was still caught
up in the dog/cat debate from earlier.
This is when everyone started making fun of me.

They were surprised I acted like that.
What kind of guy is plotting his revenge for so long regarding
such a minuscule issue?

**That was a moment when I thought I had 'won' to only
find out that I had 'lost.'**

This moment was a learning experience in regards to thin skin.
I believe sensitivity can be used for good. I call it a compass.
It can make someone aware, astute and creative.

Right before writing this story, I thought, *'hm..what should I
write about today?'*

I then said, *'thin skin.'*

Then I let my **compass** take me to a relevant memory.

However, the compass used in the wrong way can lead to the
mishap I had with Ronaq.
Bad sensitivity is when the needle of the compass is spinning in
circles which makes it hard to distinguish from north, east, south
and west.

*Controlling the compass comes down to just knowing that you
CAN control it.*

My 19 year old self automatically went in hyperdrive when that
girl disagreed with me.
Especially on a topic that I knew she knew nothing about.

It may sound like an exaggeration... But I actually thought it
was **impossible** to let that slide.
That's how my body reacted at the time.

Older me came to realize how silly that was.
Of course I could let her be wrong and go back to enjoying the
parade.

I wrote a tweet a few days ago that said something like, *'it's easier
to solve other people's problems rather than our own because
our ego is not clouding the judgment.'*

Well, that same rule applies when you're going down memory
lane.
It's like you're past self is unrecognizable to your present day self
(hopefully).

It really comes down to knowing first hand that no response is a
powerful response.
The power of ignoring is an investment to your future.

Thick skin is learned through tension and pain.
One of the hardest things to do is....nothing.
That's why so few do it.

THE UGLY ROUGH DRAFT

In this era, it's easy to get confused by the glitz and the glam.
You're seeing others on social media and thinking:
'Wow, they are so ahead of me!'

Little do you know....
They have a team behind the scenes, editing software, and tools to hide their mistakes.

You're comparing your day 1 to their day 1,160.
And that's a big mistake.

This is one reason that it's easy to undermine the importance of a rough draft.

Look around.
You see those books around you?
They were all born from a rough draft.

A rough draft is that....
Rough.

It looks ugly.
The spelling is awful.
Red lines staring at you.

But at least you have the ideas from your mind to reality.
And that's all that matters.

Writing reminds me a lot of engineering.

'It does?? They seem so different.'

Not quite, my friend.

When I was in the college of engineering, one day, my professor told me to find a regular electronic item and take it apart.

It should've been an item that I didn't use much anymore.

For some reason, like a dummy, I tore apart my AC system.

I thought I could put it back together.

But that was a little too advanced for a newbie like me!

When I tore it apart, I saw something very ugly.

Wires all over the place.

Capacitors sticking out.

Dried glue.

I was thinking:

'Ew! This looks so hideous.'

But I learned an important life lesson that day:

The engine is not always pretty.

The engine for the AC system looked like sasquatch.

But the elegant buttons, plastic encasing, the screen displaying the temperature looked beautiful.

Very similar with writing.

The rough draft looks like sasquatch.

But during editing, you clean up your mistakes, eliminate
redundant points, and sound more conversational.

Don't let all the glitz and glam fool you.

In the real world, ugly is a form of beauty.

It's because ugly is the engine that provided life for the beauty.

POWER OF GRAND GOALS

In the 90s, whenever I thought of an entrepreneur, I thought of Ted Turner.

The strangest thing was that I didn't even know what he looked like!

His name was a brand.

As I got older, I began to appreciate the dent that Ted Turner left in entrepreneurship.

He was a big thinker.

He was such a big thinker that others would usually refer to him as 'Crazy Ted.'

Ted viewed that as a compliment.

But it wasn't always like that.

Ted became a big thinker due to tragic reasons.

His father was a well renowned businessman.

He owned a lot of the billboards in high traffic areas.

And he would rent out the billboards to upcoming businesses.

Ted's father's meteoric rise in business should have been met with joy, right?

Wrong.

Ted's father felt like he reached all of his goals and now he had nothing to live for.

When Ted's father was on top of the world, he felt more
depressed than ever.

One day, Ted's father looked at him and said:

*'Son, I reached all my goals. I have nothing to live for. Be sure to
set your goals so big that you have no clue if you are going to
reach them.'*

Soon, Ted's father killed himself.

That tragic imprint turned Ted into a dog.

He went onto revolutionize industries.

From sports.

To cartoons.

To media in general.

He thought BIG.

And he moved in a way where his businesses fed of each other.

He didn't just create a cash cow in one industry.

He intertwined industries.

The idea of thinking big is a platitude nowadays.

However, it has a lot of practical benefits.

The thought waves play a large role on someone's day to day
behavior.

A big thinker flies through work.

While a little thinker needs a lot of willpower to do the tiniest of
tasks.

To be a big thinker requires tinkering.

It's highly subjective in nature.

Just because Ricky wants to own a large restaurant franchise does not mean that it's right for you.

The big thoughts should be kept a secret.

Because little thinkers are always the most vocal with giving advice and feedback.

These people are not always trustworthy.

It's not a malicious intent that is the problem.

It's the lack of information and perception that is the problem.

They look at the whole and just perceive the parts.

They see individual fingers rather than how the fingers create a palm.

Due to their limited visions, they often are very emotional and try to convince the big thinker to change strategies.

But in order to be a big thinker, you can't just be thinking all day.

You need to be moving.

Movement is what leads to thick skin.

You call a phony big thinker, 'Crazy Ted' and they will go home and cry.

But you call a real big thinker, 'Crazy Ted' and they will view it as a joke and power up some more.

One of the biggest gifts you can give someone is to help them think bigger.

But avoid making it obvious.

It should be subtle...

Humans love to buy.

But they hate to be sold to.

Likewise, humans love to think big (if it resonates with their experiences and desires).

But they hate to be lectured and force-fed commands to.

To subtly inspire them to think bigger, it can be an innocent:

'Did you ever think about....x, y and z?'

Once you ask that question, their mind begins running even when you left the room!

That's called adding value through words.

Some people are not meant to think big.

That's perfectly fine as well.

There's nothing wrong with wanting a routine life.

But others are a lion who forgot.

Now they view themselves as a house cat.

It's up to as the powerful communicator to remind the 'house cat' that they were a lion all along....

IS BEING STUBBORN BAD?

If someone comes to you and proves you wrong, then it's wise to admit that you were wrong.

That's not rocket science.

But someone with a big ego will be like:

'Yes, I'm wrong. But if X, Y, and Z were to happen... then I would've been right.'

Then they give that smug face convincing themselves they were right!!

A winner is not stubborn with these small types of moments.

But a winner is often stubborn in terms of the bigger picture.

A few years ago, I stumbled across this guy named Sam Ovens.

He covered business topics.

I thought he was refreshing.

He was coming up at a type where a lot of the business teachers were too flashy.

They had their Lamborghinis and mansions, with a sprinkle of info.

I didn't like that.

Sam on the other hand was very logical.

I noticed his transformation throughout his videos.

In the beginning of the videos, he was also flashy.

He'd wear this fancy suit and would show the view of his colossal apartment.

He seemed a bit douchey.
More on that later.

But as his videos progressed, there was a stunning transformation.
He went from looking posh to looking like a hobo.

Didn't shave.
Hair messy.
Raggedy clothes.

He explained why he did this.
It was because he wanted to focus on the content.
And focus, he did.

He talked for a long period of time without a single edit.
Showing his insane concentration.
In those long videos, he gave practical tips filled with logic.

This guy was smart.
I agreed with 98% of the things he said.
Besides 2%.

He would talk down on organic marketing a lot.
Podcasting, creating YouTube videos, and blogging.
He made it seem like it was a waste of time.

For him, Facebook ads were God.

Why invest in organic at all?

I was stunned by his serious blind spot.

Organic content are assets you own for life.
It's a brand.
It appreciates in value if you covered the right topic.

Sure, some businesses were better suited for Facebook ads.
Some were suited for a blend of paid and organic traffic.
And other businesses mainly thrived on organic.

How is someone who is smart like him not capable of seeing this?

Something in my gut told me he didn't even believe what he was saying.
More on that later.

Sam soon disappeared from YouTube.
He quit making videos and was off the grid.

In 2022, he reappeared.
He talked about his departure, what he did during that time, and his upcoming business plan.
A lot of things seemed the same.

One difference?
His newfound love for YouTube.

During his long departure, he grew somewhat resentful of Facebook ads.

CPM costs were too expensive, and Facebook was too strict with their guidelines.

But during his departure, his YouTube videos continuously bought in new leads and sold his service.

He was fascinated.

Now, he was sharing his upgraded strategy and YouTube organic marketing would be a big part of it.

I wonder how many people who agreed with most things Sam said, were misled.

I don't believe Sam misled them on purpose.

I believe he was ill informed.

I said he was dressing a little douchey in his earlier videos.

Around the same time, 'fake gurus' were on the rise.

Upcoming channels were making expose videos of popular YouTubers who seemed excessively flashy.

Multiple YouTube creators were branded fake gurus.

Sam was one of them.

I believe the backlash he received on organic traffic led him to carry a disdain towards organic traffic.

It's like a person who went through a bad breakup and now they think all relationships are poor.

Soon, they advise others to never get in a relationship.

The guys who completely altered their marketing strategy due to Sam's opinion will learn a lesson the hard way:

With some things, you have to be stubborn.

Charles Koch is a billionaire and the CEO of Koch industries.

He gets a lot of flak in the media for his political ties.

But if you listen to him, he has a lot of great insights.

One insight is that he treats his business like a scientist.

He runs a lot of experiments, gathers data, and see's what works.

He said he'd die before going public.

Why?

Because if Koch Industries was a publicly traded company, he wouldn't have the freedom to experiment like a scientist.

His shareholders would get him to focus too much on quarterly earnings, rather than the long term.

He said:

Just because numbers are easy to measure does not mean it should be measured.

Charles has stayed stubborn to his vision for 50 years!

He has remained stubborn of not going public.

I'm sure he heard a lot of advice to the contrary:

'Just go public already Charles.'

No one has the perspective of what will happen 10 years from now let alone 10 months from now.

Sometimes, stubbornness is bad.

Other times, stubbornness is another phrase for perseverance and listening to the gut

SIGNAL TO NOISE RATIO

One of the most profound engineering concepts is the signal to noise ratio.

Not only is this a fine rule to understand how communication systems work.

But it's also a great rule to understand how people work.

'What is this signal to noise ration and why should I care?'

I'm going to answer this question with a few questions of my own...

You ever had that moment when you were listening to a song on the radio?

'Yea.'

You were vibing and having a good time...?

'Yea.'

Then suddenly, the song starts to get staticky?

'Yea *sad voice*.'

After a bit, all you could hear was the static and the elegant song was a thing of the past.

-The song was the signal.

-The static was the noise.

-Signal is meaningful information.

-Noise is the junk.

A great communicator aims to build the signal and reduce the junk.

There's a basic way to do this and an advanced way to do this.

Which one do you want to hear first?

'Let's start with basic.'

The basic way to reduce the noise is by rambling less.

Rambling adds unneeded noise into other people's minds.

They don't hear the song of your voice.

They hear the static of your long windedness.

By reducing rambling and getting to the point, it's a straightforward way to reduce noise.

'Okay, then what's the advanced way to reduce noise?'

This is where things get more philosophical.

Early information theorists were confused on how to define *information*.

The founding father of Information Theory, Claude Shannon, said:

'All I need are the packets. I don't care what the packets mean.'

Claude Shannon's loose definition of information was met with a lot of backlash.

'Packets aren't the information! It's just data. Claude, you're a tittyboi!' said the other Information theorists.

The FOUNDING FATHER of information theory couldn't quite articulate what information was without being met with backlash.

The reason that relates to this email is because....

If the purpose of communication skills is to raise the Signal (meaning) and reduce static (noise), it's smart to ask:

Who determines the signal?

You ever had that moment when you outgrew friends?

The former friends were great.

But all they talked about were drugs, partying, and hookah.

You're at a new stage of your life.

Leveling up and getting into basic self-improvement.

When you try to talk to these former friends about self-improvement, they look at you with a blank face.

Is your interest of self-improvement being perceived as signal or noise by them?

'Noise?'

Unfortunately, yes.

That's why this is the advanced way to perceive the Signal to Noise ratio.

Something is advanced when it becomes nuanced.

There isn't an easy answer.

'Okay, what does that mean for me?'

It can mean a variety of things.

-Understand their interests to speak their version of a signal.

-Make your signal relatable to them. Show them how self-improvement can impact their lives.

These are just 2 of many options.

Being aware of the signal to noise ratio allows a person to become a dynamic communicator.

It helps understand why advice that works for 1 person can be dead wrong for another person.

It helps understand why it's wise to be aware of multiple fields to be an interesting personality.

And it helps understand why Susie found your joke hilarious, but Mary was offended.

As the famous saying goes:
'One man's trash is another man's treasure.'

My remix to that is:
'One man's signal is another man's noise.'

RECOGNIZING YOUR GIFTS

Encouragement is an art.

It requires precision & harmony.

There are 2 traits of encouragement:

1. A nice empowering tonality.

2. Meaningful information.

There are 2 steps in executing encouragement:

1. Listening.

2. Articulating thoughts.

I recall 2 years ago, I was going to West Palm Beach.

And I had an old friend who I didn't see in a long time mention that he was in my side of town.

He called me and said:

'Yoo, what's good man! I'm in your side of town. Wanna link up?'

I wanted to.

But I was about to head to West Palm in 2 hours.

Still had to pack.

Since I didn't see him in 2 years, I said:

'Come through man. You can help me film one of my videos.'

He didn't know what I meant.

But agreed anyways.

By the time he came, I had him record my YouTube video which was about thinking on your feet.

Once we were done, he was like:

'Yo man, that was dope! How long have you been preparing for that??'

I told him this was called impromptu speaking.

The art of thinking on your feet.

He looked back at me, puzzled.

I told him it's a skillset.

Different from planned speeches.

He looked even more confused.

That's when I gave him an example.

This friend of mine is an amazing dancer.

You want him at weddings because he knows how to create a completely different atmosphere.

Which is unusual for him.

Normally, he is to himself, quiet & shy.

However, he is gifted at dancing.

When others ask him, how long did he prepare to bust a move?

He looks back at them puzzled:

'Dude, I just follow the rhythm.'

Others (who don't dance) think he is speaking a foreign language.

But in his world, he is speaking the right language.

This guy was not always a good dancer.

He used to be really bad.

He had to work himself up to just 'follow the rhythm.'

As I used **him** as the example on how too much preparation can kill creativity, he said:

'I had no clue impromptu speaking was a thing. I've seen improv shows. But didn't know it could be systematized.

That's when he told me a story about him having to record a promo video on his IG for a company he runs.

Thus far, he hadn't shown his face.

But recently, his dad encouraged him to show his face more.

He was supposed to publish a 30 second video on an Independence Day sale he was running.

Apparently, it took him 4 hours to record the 30 second clip.

He thought I was going to be like :

'Yea right, you're exaggerating!'

But I didn't.

It's because I've seen worse.

It's because I've been worse.

We both encouraged each other.

My encouragement of his dancing was not as meaningful because his skillset was situational.

There was no wedding or big events coming up.

But his encouragement to me was meaningful.

'Man, Idk if you know this. But thinking fast like that is not easy. If you can create talks out of the ether, that's a very valuable skill man. Keep going.'

The encouragement was done in the right way.

-He said it with the right tonality.

-And the information mattered.

After that, it was all on me.

It's a game of recognizing my own gifts.

And likewise, it's a game of recognizing your own gifts.

This doesn't mean that you just say:

'Oh, I guess I got a talent. Whoopee! No more work.'

Instead, it's now a different game.

A game of:

1. Acknowledge the talent.

2. Educate yourself on the talent.

3. Fine tune the talent.

4. Use the talent to impact other people's lives.

One of my impromptu talks was on how to overcome a monotone voice.

In that talk, I introduced the One Word Game.

Where you:

SAY. ONE. WORD. AT. A. TIME.

Then you try to give each word life.

Play around with your tonalities.

Once you alter your voice on a micro level, the macro automatically changes.

The video was watched 5,000+ times.

One of the guys who watched it got my email.

And wrote me a block paragraph.

In short, he said the video resonated so much with him that he immediately began practicing.

Overtime, he noticed changes.

And people in his office noticed changes too.

Before, he was being held back in his career because his voice was boring.

It didn't spark much change & made his information sound dull.

But after building the confidence to know he could change his voice, he ran with it.

He practiced more.

The email mentioned how he got a promotion, moved his family to Texas (saved a fuck ton of money vs living in California) and is now starting a new chapter of his life.

He said my YouTube video played a significant part in his transition.

Idk the monetary gain from the promotion he received.

But what I do know is that a talent on my end, served as impact for someone else.

When acknowledging your talent, fine tune it, yes.

But see if you can take it a level further by having it make a splash in the world.

This is how you start a business while having fun at the same damn time.

For more innovative insights to changing your mindset & improving for life, be sure to check out the Level Up Mentality!

I share how to leverage fun into your self improvement journey.

Where many people quit... you just keep going and going and going.

THEORY VS APPLICATION

The way I learn:

- Get enough theory to begin.
- Begin.
- Fill in the gaps with more theory.

The way they teach in school:

- Get theory.
- Learn more theory.
- Hope that you one day get to apply.

I hated school.
Didn't like the format of education at all.

In my junior year, I was told to find a team to do a senior project with.
The senior project would be next year...
But for this year, we would choose the team and decide on an idea.

My team consisted of 2 kids named Justin and one guy named George.

We talked and talked.
Eventually, we ran into a great idea.

Let's build a smart AC!

Right now, when we used an AC, it blasted cool air into all the rooms.

It would be great if the AC only blasted air into the rooms that were occupied.

That was the idea.

How were we going to build this thing?

I don't know.

We'll find out next year once we began getting our hands dirty.

But that's not how the professor saw it.

He thought we should get a head start and create reports.

So, we had to create reports on:

- The supplies we would need.
- Our budget.
- Our deadlines etc.

I hated doing this.

All this was complete fantasy.

We don't know the answers to any of these questions until we begin applying and building.

But I understood the professor's intention.

He wanted our mind to be running in the right direction.

Also, he didn't just want us coming to class and twiddling our thumbs.

Senior year begins.

And we begin assembling the project.

**The process of turning an idea into something REAL is
one of the messiest processes out there.**

- Stuff you thought was going to be a big deal may often
  turn into a bigger deal.
- Stuff you thought was going to be light work turns out to
  be a big deal.
- And stuff you never considered...comes out of nowhere to
  be your saving grace!

Once we began building this damn thing, I was learning a lot.

Probably more than I learned in all my prior years in college of
engineering.

As we were building this thing, we had to create reports and
upload them onto a website.

This time, I didn't hate doing the reports.

I hated doing the reports earlier because it felt like we were
dabbling in fantasy.

Now, as we were building this Smart AC, writing the reports felt
like fun!

The reports were a way for the team members to crystallize our
thoughts and keep ourselves motivated.

That's when I learned:

*You learn the theory better by doing rather than learning the
theory strictly with the theory.*

When you actually do, that's when the theory isn't just dead
words on a piece of paper.

Instead, theory becomes the missing puzzle piece to the riddle you've been trying to solve!

So, if you have found yourself in analysis paralysis, remember this my friend:

'Don't be perfect, then begin.'

Instead:

'Begin, then perfect.'

This simple paradigm shift is what drives you into action.

And once you are in action, that's when you truly understand what it's like to be a learning machine.

GETTING BETTER WITH TIME

"The world around us is nonlinear, not linear."

A while back, I thought having a lot of experience meant someone was smarter.

'Isn't that the case? I thought experiences beat theory alone?'

It's not a competition.
Both complement one another.

Where experience is the cake.
Theory is the icing.

However, experience alone does not make someone street smart.
Instead, it's the enthusiasm AFTER the experience has been gained that shows street smarts.

I was pretty shocked when I saw so many lifeless people in corporate life.

Their main claim to fame was:
'Johnathan has been in this company for 20 years.'

He got handed a ribbon.
Then he complained about how he should have gotten a trophy.

Johnathan was a professional whiner and was an engineer on the side.

Despite having a lot of experience, he didn't have a glow to him.
Instead, the experience weighed him down.

I also noticed this with most barbers I've had in my life.

I used to cut hair in college for other kids in my dorm.
So I can spot a good cut from a bad cut.

I believe I have one of the easiest hairs to cut.
It's legit a combover.
A trim is all I ask for.

But I've had more bad haircuts in my life than good ones.
It's like these barbers can't follow basic directions.

After experimenting with a bunch of barbers, I finally find a guy who gives me an **amazing** haircut.
I get his name...

Then he enthusiastically does me one better and says:
'Here is my business card. I look forward to cutting your hair in the future!'

For the next few months, the barber does a great job!
I get 1 haircut per month.
Therefore, I leave a satisfied customer once a month.

After 11 months are up, that's when (like clock work) the fucking up process begins.

They have gained more experience.

And now they get content.

My last go-to guy was 45 minutes late despite me setting an appointment.

And he wreaked of weed.

After the haircut was done, he cut it too short.

And missed a spot.

It's like he completely forgot about that part.

He continued to underwhelm for the next 3 trips.

Time to find someone new...

This wasn't the first time.

I've been noticing this exact pattern for the past 6 years.

Like clockwork.

After a while, more experiences for a group of people doesn't mean a good thing

It means a toxic thing.

This is why the spirit changes when a company hires a bright eyed young kid who DOESN'T have much experience.

This bright eyed kid doesn't know what's impossible.

Therefore, in his world, everything is possible.

With that spirit, what was once impossible becomes possible!

It would be smart if the company keeps fueling that kid's optimism.

Instead, most companies completely miss the ball.

Foolishly, they have this optimistic kid proofreading a PowerPoint.

While they give the Johnathan's in the company (Mr. 20 years) more opportunities.

Despite Johnathan resenting the opportunities because he views it as 'more work.'

'What does all this imply, Armani?'

What this implies is that the process is the reward.

Experiences should add a glow to your eyes.

You should be feeling more FIRE after each rep.

Because each rep done correctly leads to more knowledge.

Knowledge leads to refining the process.

The process is the reward.

The reason a lot of these people with experience become dead in the eyes is because they don't view the process like that.

'Why not?'

Because they have a linear view of reality.

In their mind, they are running a race.

At the end, there is a ribbon that they need to run through.

Therefore, the entire running process, they are like:

'Lets get this over with already!!'

While a nonlinear system view of the world is entirely different.

Think about the attitude you have when you eat.

A person who hasn't eaten ALL day doesn't look at the feast in front of them with the attitude of:

'Okay lets get though this already. I want to wince in pain in front of the tv after I eat this feast.'

They are the most excited about the EATING part!

The eating is the reward!!

This is the mindset of someone who enjoys the process.

It's a different philosophy entirely.

This is what I break down in the Level Up Mentality book.

I logically explain why it's smarter to view the mind as a nonlinear information system rather than a linear one.

2 ways for an information system to progress:

1. Create value.

2. Connect value.

These people who are looking older and more depressed after their experiences are not enjoying the process.

Therefore, they are **not** street smart.

The only way someone builds street smarts is by:

1. Gaining real world experience.

2. Cultivating more enthusiasm over time.

That's what connecting value is.

It's when knowledge alters energy levels.

Energy is something everyone wants more of.

No one wakes up in the morning and says:
'Geez, I want to be tired for the rest of the day!'
They wonder how they can feel more **alive**.

Well, view the process as the reward.

Gain more experience (value).

Connect those value to new information & new experiences.

Build energy.

A complex system lowers it's entropy and builds more life.

That's how you get better with time.

SYSTEMS THINKING

Systems thinking is going to be revolutionary.

More people are going to talk about it as the world builds in complexity.

Textbooks are going to be written on the topic.

Experts will emerge.

Scholars will defend their new theories.

I think all that will be a waste of time.

'Why?? How else am I going to learn systems thinking?'

Through storytelling.

Systems thinking is seeing the interconnections among the nodes.

Nodes are parts.

Interconnection is how the nodes work together (aka: the process).

Few examples of a system.

Your palm....

Fingers are the nodes.

All of them working together create the palm.

Another example is your car.

Steering wheel, mirrors, engine, etc.

Alone, they mean nothing.

When they are intertwined, they create the car.

Another example of a system is **you**.

Thoughts, feelings, hair, eyes, skin separately mean nothing.

Heck, it can be borderline gross.

But all those intertwined creates you, the person.

'Why are you saying storytelling helps with systems thinking?'

Because the act of storytelling teaches you how everything is connected.

A tiny detail from chapter 2 becomes the plot twist for chapter 19.

The audience member is shocked.

While the storyteller was capable of perceiving the plot twist all along.

A great way to get started is by telling stories about yourself.

In the land of lessons, time doesn't exist.

A lesson that you learned in age 5 can impact you at age 25, 45 and 65.

When I was 5, I remember talking a lot of shit to this kid who was double my size.

He was normally soft spoken.

I kept roasting him.

Said he looked like Fat Albert.

A few of us were chilling by my place outside.

He told me to quit plenty of times.

But I continued anyway.

After some time, he beat me up.

I was livid.
Couldn't do anything because he was so much bigger.

Next day, we were at the bus stop, and he tried to apologize.
I was too pissed to accept his apology & shooed him away.

There was another friend next to me named Bowley who asked why I waved him off?
That's when I told Bowley about how I got beat up.

Bowley was even smaller than me.
But he was ready to fight this big guy to seek revenge for me.

He walks to the guy who beat me up and was like:
*'You hit my boy Armani?! Fuck you! Armani didn't do **anything** to deserve that. Fight me, let's go!!'*

As Bowley was sticking up for me, that's when I realized my error.
When Bowley said that I didn't do anything wrong, I realized that I did do something wrong.

I was the one provoking him.
He told me to stop plenty of times.
Then he responded how he responded.

This incident taught me a bunch of lessons.
Here are a few:

-In the real world, everyone doesn't resolve conflict with words, they do so with fists.

-Self awareness is difficult to build. But when an insight hits, it hits hard.

-Acting like a victim feels good because it deflects blame.

Mind you, this incident was from age 5!
Yet, these lessons still impact me to this day.

Through storytelling, the mind starts to think in systems.

Systems thinking will become more popular.
Reductionism alone will no longer cut it.

Stay tuned for tomorrow, I'm going to run a free deal for my new book, **Cobra: A Story on Social Anxiety, People Skills, Leadership and Greatness.**

I'll drop more details on the book tomorrow.
Peace.

DELAYED DEPRESSION?

I had this strange memory from a few years ago when a friend invited me to get Boba tea with him.

He lived in Miami.
I lived in Tampa.

We were cool in undergrad, but after he moved, we didn't keep in touch like that.
There wasn't bad blood or anything.

He was like:
'Yo man, you trying to get Boba tea? It's on me. I'm in Tampa.'

I was pretty busy so I declined.

That's when he said:
'It'll only be 30 minutes man. Kinda important.'

He was normally a laid back guy.
So if he said it was important, then it was important.

Told him to pick me up from the library & I was down.
He was one of my Haitian buddies.

By the time we are getting Boba, I ask him what's good.
What was so urgent?

That's when he starts sort of crying talking about:

'I miss Noajah bro....'

Noajah? I thought.

This fool dated Noajah in high school. And he graduated college at this point. I asked him if he was referring to the same girl.

He nodded his head.

That's when I asked:

'Bro, it's been YEARS that y'all have been broken up. Why are you randomly sad now?? lmao.'

I started laughing.
Thought he was joking.

But he wasn't joking.
It was pretty serious.

He told me he acted out of character and visited her in Atlanta, unannounced.
He said lately, he was feeling depressed.
When she saw him show up, she was shocked.
Told him not to visit again.

As I talked to this Haitian buddy, he introduced the concept of "delayed depression" to me.
He said he normally feels sad about something WAY after it happens.

I thought that was unique.
Also, it allowed me to see how emotions work differently for different people.

Having the foresight to deal with a scenario like this always keeps the mind in learning mode.

-A fixed mind thinks they know everything.

-A growth mind knows they can have 1 experience that shifts their view of reality.

In my new book:

Cobra: A Story on Social Anxiety, People Skills, Leadership and Greatness

The main character, Cobra, wonders if he is depressed.

His mom left him, dad committed suicide, and girlfriend cheated on him with his best friend.

He heard about depression before.

But has no clue if he has it.

There's a lady that can help him....

Maybe.

That's his teacher.

The story of Cobra teaches how to use dark moments to be like the arrow.

An arrow is pulled back before it is propelled forward.

It seems like everything is falling apart...

For you to only realize everything was falling right into place.

HAZING

On the first day of my first internship, my manger, John, walks me into the cube.

He sets me up in the cube and then leaves.

Once he leaves, I felt confused.

Um... what do I exactly do?

It was my first day, so I was clueless.

Do I start surfing the web?

Read some documents??

Just sit there???

I was stuck.

As a few minutes go by, I hear a lady in the cube across from me talking to a man.

I wasn't trying to eavesdrop, but they were so close to me.

As I heard the words, I could make out what they were saying.

They were talking shit about me!!

'You heard we got a new intern? I don't even know why they are wasting money on an intern. Maybe they could try giving us a raise.'

'Yea, I hear the intern is going to be getting the same cube size as us.'

'Let's hope this intern knows something. The last one was an idiot.'

I was surprised.

This was my first ever brush with a 40 hour a week role.

I was expecting more professionalism.

They were talking crap so openly too, as if they were not even trying to hide it.

A few minutes later, John comes back and is like:

'Let me introduce you to the others on the floor.'

He introduces me to a few people.

Then he takes me to the cube of the 2 who were talking shit about me.

We go into the cube and see 2 people.

One Asian woman in her 40s named Amy.

One Haitian man in his 40s named Jean.

John tells Amy and Jean that I am the new intern and that I was going to be sitting **right across** from them.

Then he points to the cube for more of a comedic effect!

When they found out that I was in the cube right across from them when they were bad mouthing me....

They looked like they were shitting bricks!!

They never apologized.

Nor did I expect an apology.

But they gave me the face of:

'Sorry about that.'

I was used to this kind of treatment.

Whenever I joined a new organization before, there was a hazing phase.

My definition of hazing is:

-Putting a new recruit/member through a weeding out process to test their desire.

The hazing phase is typically associated with fraternities.

Where the fraternity puts the new recruits through a mentally and physically grueling process.

Other times, hazing doesn't happen with fraternities, it happens in a work environment.

This type of hazing is much more subtle...

Example:

It normally takes 1 hour to get an approval on a document for a veteran member. But for the newbie member, it takes the entire day to get an approval.

'Why do you think that is?'

Because the old school members are seeing if the new members are congruent to who they say they are.

Different people will have different opinions regarding hazing.

Some will hold the opinion:

-*Well, it's just a part of our culture.*

Others will hold the opinion:

-It's time to eliminate hazing for good.

I see a case for both sides.

However, I am realistic.

I understand that hazing is a weeding out process.

Rather than saying:

'Why me?'

It would be smarter to say:

'Hazing is a part of a bunch of different industries. Rather than whining about it so fast, I'll only allow it to power me up some more.'

I can't even imagine what would have happened if I snitched on Amy and Jean.

If I did that, I'm sure John would have disciplined them.

But how much would that have thrown off the **vibe** of the internship process??

Amy and Jean would have given me a cold shoulder because I was a snitch.

Instead, not even bringing it up and showing enthusiasm despite the disrespect allowed them to take me under their wings.

When you're new to a field, having thick skin makes it much easier to assimilate into the culture.

Amy was the software engineer.

Jean was the hardware engineer.

Throughout my next few months there, they went out of their way to teach me a lot.

Hazing may suck in the beginning stages.

Sometimes, you may need to get authorities involved if you are dealing with a tyrant.

But a lot of other times, it's harmless.

It's a subtle process that many industries follow to this day.

Use it to strengthen you.

And you'll enjoy having passed the weeding out process once you make it to the end.

VULNERABLE PEOPLE

A few years ago, I knew 2 girls named Nisreen and Alicia.

I knew Nisreen liked me.
But I knew Alicia hated me.
They were both best friends.

'Why did Alicia hate you?'
No clue.

One weekend, there was a party being hosted in Orlando.
I needed a ride.

There was a guy who said his car was packed but had room for 1 more person.
That one person was me.

When I arrived at the meeting location, I saw Nisreen with 2 other girls.
Nisreen was pleasantly surprised to see me there.
She didn't know I was going to be in the same car as her.

But unfortunately, I saw Alicia too.

Immediately, Alicia starts making sarcastic comments:
'Ah...Arman's coming with us? Just when I thought tonight was supposed to be a good night.'

She had this sassy personality.

I'm one of those guys who hates sassiness and sarcasm.

Others may like it, but that's never been my thing.

I'm sitting in the passenger seat and playing music.

As I'm playing music, the other passengers are loving it.

All besides...

You guessed it.

Alicia.

'Do you only listen to rap? Why can't you play some rock?' she said.

Who the hell listens to rock music before going to a party??

By the time we were in Orlando, I tried to spend more time with Nisreen.

But Alicia kept following us & cockblocking.

Despite me not liking her, Alicia was pretty.

Other guys would try to talk to her at the party.

But her attitude was so bad that it made her unbearable.

Eventually, the guys would dip & she would follow me and Nisreen around some more.

By the end of the night, the guy who initially drove us was black out drunk.

That meant that I need to drive us back.

I gathered everyone, got in the car & proceeded to drive on the night highways...

After an hour in a half, we were back to Tampa.

That's when I notify Alicia, Nisreen & the 3rd girl that we are in front of their apartment.

Only problem.

'What?'

Alicia wasn't getting up.

She was black out drunk.

We tried getting her to wake up for some time.

But it was futile.

At that point, the other 2 girls looked at me like they knew our only option.

I had to *carry* Alicia to her place.

This was a 5 storied building.

Plus, the elevators were not working.

I'd have to carry her up 5 stories, while I'm wearing dress shoes and my fresh jeans too!

Did I mention that I hit legs at the gym earlier in the day??

I looked at Alicia in disgust and saw there was no other option.

The other 2 girls were too small to pick her up.

I took Alicia out the car, swung her over my shoulder &
proceeded to walk up the flight of stairs.

These were one of those buildings where there was
a *long* walkway before you got to the next flight of steps.

You climb one flight of stairs.

Then you walk on a flat floor for some time.

Then you roll around and take the next flight of stairs.

Eventually, I made it to their apartment and dropped Alicia off to
her bed.

The other girls thanked me.

3 weeks passes by...

One day, I'm at a club.

I see a bunch of familiar faces.

Unfortunately, one of those familiar faces was Alicia.

I was going to ignore her like I usually do.

But she grabbed my forearm and said:

'Thank you.'

I said, *'all good,'* and was about to leave.

That's when she was like:

'Let me buy you a drink.'

I was like *'nah, I'm all good. I'm the D.D.'*

She said:

'Let me buy you a Coke then.

'Nah, I'm dieting. All good, don't mention it.'

For the next couple of years, Alicia became my brand ambassador.

We had a lot of friends in common.

I would hear from them how she'd always talk me up.

Her sassy attitude began to die down and she became sweeter around me.

Alicia taught me an important lesson in the social skills world.

'Which was?'

One of the best times to do a favor for someone is when they are vulnerable.

Vulnerable = Stuck in an Embarrassing Moment

Let's say a proud man suddenly got a DUI & doesn't have the funds to pay for the lawyers.

This guy reaches out to you, and you have more than enough money.

If you help them at that moment, it's one of those things that will win you a supporter for a long... long time...

A while back, I used to donate plasma.

This was a quick way to make some extra pocket change.

One day, I was notified I had a few parking tickets that I needed to pay asap.

I didn't have the funds to pay for those tickets.

Your boy didn't know what to do.

I was letting a buddy of mine know about the issue.

I wasn't even asking him to pay it, was just thinking out loud.

That's when he said:

'If you pay me back in a timely manner, I'll take care of your payments.'

I ended up getting my plasma check in a few days, so he never needed to pay my bills.

But just knowing that he was **willing** to pay made me his brand supporter.

During moments of vulnerability, the sassy turn sweet.

The proud turn humble.

And enemies ask for help.

This is the primal way to build support.

COMMUNICATIONS WEB

I had a buddy who worked with Brian Tracy a few years ago.

He joined Brian Tracy's mastermind and met up with him in California to meet the group & learn.

During that trip, one of his takeaways was that Brian Tracy was a great speaker (duh).

But not only was he a great speaker, he was a great writer too.

Brian Tracy is a prolific note taker.

His note taking skills apparently make it easier for him to create speeches at will.

A few days after the Brian Tracy event, this buddy of mine began networking in Tampa to meet more speakers.

He asked them for tips.

One of the speakers said:

'If I could start all over, I would have begun writing sooner.'

The speaker didn't give advice that talked about speaking.

Instead, it delved into writing.

Why?

My buddy said that the prolific note taking practice helped him create speeches on demand.

It was easier to recall information.

Today, as I was coming back from West Palm Beach, I stopped at a gas station in the middle of nowhere to pick up an energy drink.

As I go to pick up the energy drink, the gas station had a few people in it.

No one seemed to stick out....

Besides the guy next to me.

The guy next to me was in his late 30s, wearing shorts and a blue long sleeve shirt with sunglasses on his head.

He was with his wife and 3 kids.

I look at this guy and am like:

'This dude looks just like JJ Barea.'

JJ was an NBA player who won a championship with the Dallas Mavericks.

That team was well known for beating the 'Heatles' aka the Miami Heat team with LeBron James, Chris Bosh, and Dwyane Wade.

Then I thought:

'Nah. What would JJ Barea be doing at this dusty gas station in the middle of nowhere?'

I asked him:

'Yo man, are you JJ Barea?'

He proudly nodded his head & stuck out his hand to shake my hand.

I was like:

'Whoa, no way!! Can I take a picture with you?'

He agreed to take the pic.

After the pic, I thought:

'He seems very small on TV. But in real life, he's way bigger.'

He's 5 foot 10, which is really short for an NBA player.

He is often towered by the other players.

But in person, he didn't seem small.

I'm sure you have heard the phrase:

-The camera adds 5 pounds.

My remix to that is:

-The camera takes away 5x your presence.

A guy whose power you can FEEL in real life may not be as noticeable on camera.

But when you see him in real life, you are like:

'Whoa, that guy was different.'

Just like Brian Tracy complements notes with speaking...

I think another useful trick is to complement YouTube with speaking.

If you are someone who routinely has to present at work for a meeting or lead weekly calls...

A content creation practice will complement and help.

So you're not sitting idle as you wait to speak again.

Instead, you keep the momentum going with a content creation practice.

Also, you'll feel less performance anxiety when you are called to give a talk.

At first, you may be like:

'What the hell does speaking on camera have to do with speaking in real life?'

Until you try speaking on camera & notice a significant difference in your speaking game in real life.

The **micro muscles** you build speaking on camera spills over to on-stage!

Each person is different.

What works for one person may fall flat for another person.

For example, I'm not a big note taker.

However, I am a prolific writer.

I write blogs, tweets and newsletters a lot.

You may be like:

'I'm not writing a newsletter or blog every day, that's overkill!.

But you may end that sentence with:

'However, the notetaking doesn't sound too bad. I guess I can write some notes on that notepad app I have on my phone.'

Communication skills seem separate at first.

In the beginning state, it doesn't seem like writing can help with speaking.

Or that speaking can help writing.

Or that writing can help with podcasting.

But overtime, you'll notice all these skillsets gluing into 1 big web.

The more that you create the web, the more creative, unpredictable & prolific that you become.

It's a process.

The process is what makes each person's communication style unique.

BEING RESOURCEFUL

"I did so much with so little that I can do anything with something...."

This was a quote I heard a while back that reminded me of what it took to be resourceful.

I noticed streets smarts people are highly resourceful.

They don't have much.

However, they are able to do a lot.

It's difficult, if not impossible, to do a lot when a person is a perfectionist.

Being a perfectionist masks fear.

'What you mean? I'm a perfectionist and I'm not fearful at all!'

Look deeper....

Emotions often exist in layers.

What meets the eye isn't the full truth.

A perfectionist may convince themselves:

'No sir, I just need a perfect product, nothing to fear.'

That mindset may work, if they actually release something.

But if they keep working & never hitting publish... fear is around the corner.

'What kind of fear?'

The fear of being judged.

It sucks to be judged when you could have perfected it even more.
And someone notices the *same* thing that you noticed when you were being a perfectionist.

Let's say a painter needs a special kind of paint.
However, that special kind of paint won't arrive for 3 weeks.

They have an art show *today*.
So, the painter uses what they have.

In the paint show, tons of people congratulate the painter's art.
However, 1 person notices that the painter could have used the special paint.

The perfectionist painter is crushed.
A stadium full of compliments gets drowned out by 1 criticism.

This is the mindset of a lot of perfectionists.
That fear of being noticed for their deficiency influences their moves.

Procrastination will never get you started.
Perfectionism will never get you finished.

Resourcefulness is built when you have very little.
This is when you're bootstrapping everything from the beginning.

This is a real world class on street smarts.
And you are the principal, student, guidance counselor etc.

The reason that communication skills allow a person to be resourceful is because it comes in handy, simple as that.

When you already have little finances, the ability to negotiate a price from $500 to $425 does wonders.

The guy who built my website was going to charge me 5000 dollars.

I got it down to $2500.

That 2500 dollars saved allowed me to invest in the web server, write a few books, invest in the covers etc.

I didn't try to rip this guy off.

Instead, I introduced him to many more clients.

He eventually made all his money back from the business I referred.

All that began with strategically placing the words together to create a negotiation deal.

Words are free.

Are you resourceful?

If not, you may be suffering from perfectionism.

If you are suffering from perfectionism, rather than wearing it as a badge of honor....

Ask:

'What am I afraid of?'

This question will lead to a meaningful answer.

That meaningful answer will officially begin your School of Hard Knocks.

That's how street smarts is built.

LEARNING FROM THE PAST

There was one night I saw an odd-looking lady at Walmart with 2 little girls.

She looked like an Amish woman.

I've seen people like that on TV before.

But never saw one in person.

I was just getting out of the gym.

I went to the Walmart to buy a protein shake.

Was going to buy it, drink it, then go home.

As I'm waiting in line behind her, she **suddenly** turns around and looks at me.

Then she angrily asks:

'Did you steal my 20 dollars?'

She asks it loud enough where a few heads turn.

Others began looking at me suspiciously.

To make matters worse, I normally look like a goon going to the gym.

I wear a big black hoodie.

Where the hoodie over my head.

And after the gym, I feel tired, so I rest my hands in the front pocket of the jacket.

Other customers began looking at me like:

'Well, his hands are in the front pocket. If he stole the 20 dollars, I know where he put the money!'

I tell the lady:
'Nah, I didn't steal your money.'

But the lady pressed further.
She's like:
'Are you sure? I know I had 20 dollars on me.'

I once again said I didn't steal her money.

She once again looks back at me and says:
*'I **know** I had 20 dollars on me.'*

Then she follows up with:
'Can I see you empty your pockets?'

The cashier looks at me with the stink eye.
Now others are looking at me like:
'Just do it...If you didn't steal it, you should be good.'

This infuriated the younger me.
After a gym session, I'm tired.
Now I have this bitch interrogating me.

I didn't want a problem.
Just wanted the protein shake so I could get out of there.
Judging by the lady's demeanor, I could sense she would have been okay calling the cops and dragging this on.

I empty my pockets.

Show her there wasn't a 20-dollar bill in my wallet.
I had a few dollar bills and some change.

As I'm showing her proof, I look back at the lady and say:
'I'd double check your purse if I were you.'

She had this big ass purse too!

As she goes through it again....
Looky looky!!
She makes eye contact with her 20 dollars.

She abruptly turns around, looks at the cashier and hands him the money.
Never even apologized to me.

When she didn't apologize to me, it made me really angry.
I wanted to curse her out and tell her to be more cautious before accusing people like that.

The other dummies who were looking at me suspiciously in line now had the face of:
'I knew the black hoodie boy was innocent!'

During that period, I was pissed.
Nowadays, I find that memory funny.

Annoying moments from the past become funny moments of the present...
Only if an insight is drawn.

That's what it means when someone says:
'You need to forgive the person.'
Or
'You need to move on.'

'Forgiving' and 'moving on' are not simple commands.
It's a process.

And the process is to draw a lesson from the experience.

No matter how annoying the experience, there is a silver lining buried within.

'What was the lesson you learned from that moment?'
I didn't learn a lesson.
I learned lessons.

Few included:

1. Be extra wary before accusing someone of something.

2. If you are going to accuse someone, and you happen to be wrong, be loud with the apology.

3. Know both sides of the story before taking sides.

And much more.

Once I learned the lessons, which presented itself over time, it allowed the memory to be funny.

I actually told this story at a Toastmasters meeting once and got a bunch of laughs.

How does a gold watch business work?

1. They extract raw gold from land.

2. Then the process that raw gold to turn it into gold watches.

3. Then they distribute the gold watches to the customer.

How does a modern storyteller work?

1. They extract raw experiences from their memory.

2. Then they process (introspect) the raw experiences into stories.

3. Then they distribute those stories to audience members through speeches, podcasts, and writings.

Storytelling and maturing go hand in hand.

IS THE DEAL NEEDED?

One of the questions you want to ask before negotiating with someone is:

-Is this deal needed?

Actually, scratch that...

Ask:

-Is this deal **NEEDED**?

By doing this, you're capable of scoping through a lot of fluff.

Plus, it allows you to factor in variables that you initially didn't consider.

Imagine that you have a great client in terms of finances.

They always pay on time.

However, they have an issue.

'What's that?'

They are a hot head.

They yell at you and put you down a lot.

Sure, they are giving you the money.

But in terms of servicing them... it's becoming a headache.

Before you negotiate your next plan with them, ask:

-Is this deal **NEEDED**?

This allows you to factor in your emotional side as well.

You may think:

'Hm... no, not really. I have a lot of other leads. I don't know why I have such a scarcity mindset towards clients. This guy needs to go!'

This insight would not have been noticed if you went straight into negotiating.

My first time realizing this was in college.

I recall I was getting back from a party.

My friend was dropping me off.

Once he dropped me off, he was like:

'It'd be cool if we were business partners.'

I was like:

'Yea, it would be.'

Then I was about to leave.

But before I left...

I had an idea.

Why don't we get free stuff from Craigslist and sell it for some money?

I ran the idea by him and he was all in.

We began talking about how the whole operation would work.

Mind you...

I didn't have a car, and he had a tiny car.

Plus, we barely had money to rent a truck.

Still, we were talking away as if we had a deal in the making.

If we simply asked:

-Is the deal **NEEDED**?

We'd probably had an aha moment.

I would have probably thought:

'No, not right now. My grades aren't the best, and even scouring through Craigslist seems like a pain. Even if we do find a nice free product, what if it's big and we can't fit it in the tiny car?'

That would have saved a conversations and I could've saved a few extra hours of sleep.

The thing is...

Nowadays, it's easier to communicate with others.

Soon as you have some scale, people are coming into your DMs pitching their services.

They are pitching themselves too.

And if you are just saying yes to everyone, then you have overhead in the making.

This is for business.

This is for relationships.

Therefore, the next time you are about to negotiate ask:

-Is the deal **NEEDED**?

Soon, you will spot the "must have deals" from the "pleasant to have deals."

Annoying to Funny

A few days ago, my mic stopped working.
The mic that I recorded podcasts on.

The next day, I was going to have a podcast interview.
I needed to get a mic **fast**.

I go to Best Buy and ask them for a mic.
Each of the workers were clueless.
They could barely answer any questions and seemed aggravated that they were being bothered.

I finally met this elderly worker who was willing to help.
Despite being willing to help, he didn't have good news for me.

The mic that I wanted was out of stock.
He said it would be delivered till tomorrow at 6 pm.
My interview was tomorrow at 11 am.

I check Amazon.
Surprisingly, I see good news.

The mic was available for overnight delivery.
The latest it would show up was 9-10 am tomorrow.
Great, I placed the order and slept l like baby.

The next morning, I am waiting for the mic.
By the time I check Amazon orders, it writes:

'Package has been delivered.'

For real?
I didn't hear anyone knock.
I opened my door and see my welcome mat.
But no mic...

What the hell?
Did they deliver to the wrong address??
Dammit!

I gave them a call and got a support agent who seemed to be having a bad day.
Normally, I get top quality service from Amazon, but this guy seemed out of it.

He said the package needed to be refunded.
I told him that the mic was **just** "delivered."
So the mail man was not too far away.
I asked if he could call the mail man.

I know this used to be possible (not sure of it still is) because I had a scenario like this happen a year ago.

But this guy said it was not possible.
I tried to get him to do further research, but no lie...
He hung up on me!

I got pissed.
Called back.
This time, a woman picks up and she seems very enthusiastic.

I explain my scenario and she was like:

'I normally can't give out the mail man's info, but today, I'll give access.'

She connected me with the mail man.

I explained the scenario to him.

He recites my address and said he dropped it off there.

Clearly he made a mistake!

I ask him, what now?

He says:

'I'm sorry, son. I'm out of the area. But if you'd like to find the mic, look for a pineapple.'

A pineapple??

That's when he asked me to check my mail.

I should've gotten the picture of the door that the package was dropped off to.

So, I check my mail and notice the picture.

The door has a picture of a pineapple.

Clue number 1.

Now the question was:

Where the hell is this door??

I do what any sane person would do.

I look for the cops.

I'm sure the police officers know this area very well, they should be able to identify the door!

There is a place right by me where 2 police officers are always standing.
I never go into the parking lot area, I only walk by it.
But today, I would be driving in there.

The parking lot is really tricky.
You need to make a lot of twists and turns to reach the officers.
When they see me pulling in, I see one of them touch their gun.
They don't pull it out or anything.

But it was a sudden body language move like:
'Who is this strange man driving towards us?'

When I pull up, I noticed this area was some sort of day care area.
That's why the cops looked at me with caution.
They probably thought:
'Who the hell is this adult driving in a day care area?'

I'm not making the best impression...

I show them the photo of the door, and they both take a look.
Both shake their heads and say they've never seen the door before.

Damn...
What now?

I pull up Google maps and begin to type in the beginning of my address and see what auto populates.

I drove to all those addresses.

I went to the hood.

Drove to an apartment complex.

And drove to another hood.

No pineapple.

At this point, I was getting pissed.

There had to be a way.

Suddenly, I had a flash of an idea.

I recall there were a few times the Uber Eats driver dropped my food off at the wrong place.

I recall the last order that was botched.

I pull up the order receipt from the app.

That's when I see the mistaken address that my Uber driver went to.

I pull it up on my phone and notice it's literally WALKING distance from where I live.

Here I was, driving all over the place, but this area was **right** next to me.

I went up to the new location.

I walked up the drive way.

That's when I see a pineapple looking my way.

I found it!!!

I saw this guy working on a house, fixing some stuff.
I asked him if he lived in the pineapple house.
He shook his head.

I asked him if he knew who lived in pineapple house.
He nodded his head.

He pointed to a woman getting out of her car.
It was this 30ish year old woman named Patty.
She wore braces, was white, and had brown hair.

I was way bigger than her, so I wanted to be as unthreatening as possible.
I walked up to her, introduced myself and said that I believed my package was delivered to her place.

She found the whole ordeal funny.
She went to her door, and from behind this cardboard box, found my white package!

I then joked;
'You must get a lot of random Uber Eats meals delivered to your place.'
She laughed and said she did.

That day, I learned that annoying moments make for the funniest stories.

If I wrote an email talking about how I got my mail and everything went well, you'd be like:

'So?'

You wouldn't find it interesting.

It wouldn't be interesting because there was no *uncertainty* in the story.

But when *uncertainty* is introduced to the mix...then the whole dynamic changes.

Now the story becomes entertaining.

It's difficult to keep the bigger viewpoint in mind when the annoying thing is happening... because we don't know what the result will be.

After the cops incident, I thought the mic was a lost cause.

But once I was walking back to my place with the bag in my hand, I viewed the entire situation as funny.

So, when you are going through an annoying moment, simply introduce a tiny gap in thinking with the statement:

'This may end up being a hilarious story for my future self.'

That tiny gap in thinking changes the narrative entirely.

And you will reduce the likelihood of acting out.

BEYOND CONTROL

There are different types of posts in this newsletter.

-Some are stories from my past.

-Some are things that I noticed.

Today's post will be a blend of the 2.

I recall in my final year of high school, there was a girl named Becky.

She was dating this guy named Robert.

They were a very strange looking couple.

Becky was this tall girl with **really** big ears. She would wear pigtails which highlighted how big her ears were.

Robert was this stumpy looking guy.

He wasn't fat, but definitely wasn't skinny either.

Becky was 6 foot.

Robert was around 5'4.

Although the couple looked strange, they grew on the school students.

They were one of the few couples in Forest Hill High.

Others eventually viewed them as a:

'Cute couple.'

They got along well for a while.

Until eventually, Robert was caught cheating on her.

He cheated on her with a girl from our IB program named
Chelsea.

The IB program was an accelerated program that helped you get
ready for college earlier.

The IB community was small.

There were 4 boys and 9 girls.

When Chelsea was identified as the homewrecker who broke up
the strange looking 'cute' couple, it was easy to identify her.

*"She's one of the girls from the IB program! Can't trust those IB
kids,"* the school would gossip.

Never before did the IB program have this much attention.

It was a strange time for us.

It was a stranger time for Becky..

To make matters worse, there was a song that came out around
that time called Becky by Plies.

If you haven't heard the song, it's pretty much about getting head.

So, Becky just got cheated on.

And now her name was synonymous for oral sex.

**I thought of her recently when I realized some things
are beyond your control and you have no choice but to
ride the waves out.**

Becky was able to ride the waves out.

She seemed cordial when she brushed past Robert and Chelsea
holding hands.

Nowadays, I wonder how it feels to be a woman named Karen.

Karen is becoming an adjective for someone who makes a big deal out of ordinary situations.

It must be tough to be a Karen who has supreme patience.

You wake up one morning, and your name is a meme.

Point being, there are a lot of things that happen beyond our control.

This is something to think about when you are going through a strange time and are like:

'I didn't do anything to deserve this.'

These moments happen to everyone.

Not only you.

When you forget that, recall the story of Becky for added perspective.

Then ride out the waves...

CARING

A couple years back, I moved to Virginia for a job.
For me, this was the middle of nowhere.

Younger me thought...
Who the fuck lives in Virginia?

And more specifically, I thought..
Who the fuck lives in Sterling Virginia?

I was a clueless kid in his early 20s who spent most of my life in Florida.

The job was to work in an IT company.
And in the initial stages, the company was going to provide me housing.

There was going to be this thing called a **boarding house.**
Where a lot of the trainees would stay.

Basically, there was a new batch of trainees every 60 days.
As the prior class of trainees left, the new ones would come to occupy the house.

On the day I flew from Florida to Virginia, my flight had gotten delayed many times.

After **hours** of waiting, the plane finally came.
And I was ready for a new chapter.

I arrived in Virginia late at night.
And was hungry as shit.

To make matters worse, my taxi driver was a newbie.
He didn't know the area too well & wanted me to give him directions.
I told him I was new here.

After fumbling around the streets for a while, he finally pulls up into the luxury neighborhood.

COLOSSAL houses.

I thought this idiot taxi driver pulled up in the wrong location.
Thought he was intentionally acting clueless to run up the
charges.

But no....
He was in the right spot.

Sterling Virginia is no regular spot.
It's one of the richest areas of all of America.
And the boarding house was in one of the most expensive
neighborhoods.

My company gave me a key.
I went in.
Finally, some warmth.

This was a 3 storied house.
I heard a bunch of chatter on the second floor as I walked in.
After putting my suitcases down on the first floor, I walked
upstairs.

There were at least 6 people there.
4 girls and 2 guys.
A few were Nepali, a few were Indian & 1 girl was Haitian.

They looked at me like I was some kind of burglar.

So I quickly introduced myself as the new roommate of theirs.
All of them introduced themselves to me.
Then went back to chatting in their clique.

I asked them if there was a room for me to stay?
And one of them said:
*'All the rooms are taken. But one of the members will be out by
next week. So you can have the room then! Till then, you have to
stay in the basement.'*

Now let me be clear.
The basement is not some dark disgusting spot that is often
pictured.
The basement for this house looked like another living room.

Looked awesome!

Only thing was that there wasn't a bed.
I would have to sleep on the couch for the week.

As I go to the basement, my stomach starts growling.
I'm hungry as fuck.

I didn't have the money to be spending it on a taxi back and forth.
Needed to properly budget till I got my first paycheck.
(New employees didn't get paid until their training was up).

So I go downstairs and began settling down.
Unpacking.

As I am unpacking, I hear footsteps walking down.

A guy in his 30s.
Short.
Bearded.
Wearing informal clothes came to me.

*'My bad, I was upstairs when you came. I'm Ali. Are you the
new roommate?'*
I responded yes.

Ali was holding a fried chicken meal box.
It smelled good.
Seemed like he had just picked it up.

We chatted for a few on the couch.
Then abruptly, he asks me for my number.
I gave it to him.

After he took my number, he excused himself to go upstairs.
However, he left his fried chicken meal downstairs.

I didn't initially notice he left the box because I was still exploring
the basement.

Then I get a text shortly.
*'Hey, I'm not that hungry. You can have my chicken box meal. I
just got it, so it's unopened.'*

Damn.
You don't have to tell me twice!!

I ate that.
And it felt like one of the best meals I had in a while.

FOR THE NEXT COUPLE OF MONTHS, ALL THE ROOMMATES AND I WERE GETTING ACCLIMATED.

I got to know more about Ali.
He was a badass from the way he described himself.
A former marine who killed people.

I thought he was just a good storyteller.
But he showed me a lot of pictures of him in the Middle East in his uniform.

Ali had a compelling background.
Homeless, reunited with his brother after years, fought in wars and much more.

He was a very tough guy.
Plus, you could tell he wanted to be perceived as tough.

-When all the other roommates would laugh, Ali would remain stone faced.
-When people were joking too much, he'd bring us back to reality.
-When people got lazy with household chores, he'd let us know.

One day, one of the other roommates, Samiksha, asked me to help her move her TV upstairs.
As I helped her move, we began talking.

Somehow, Ali came up.
She said:
'Don't let Ali fool you. He's one of the softest hearted guys you'll ever meet. He just doesn't like showing it.'

I asked in intrigue, oh yea??

Then she told me about my first night.
'You know the first night you moved in? How he gave you his fried chicken meal? He hadn't eaten all day. But he gave it to you without second thought because he thought you may be hungry.'

When she told me that, I was very surprised.
And very touched.
That was a very kind move.

I thought he wasn't hungry when he gave me that.
But Samiksha's backstory changed my perception.

It made sense why he texted me rather than give it to me face to face.
He didn't want to be perceived as soft.
He wanted to be perceived as tough...

Ali and I still keep in touch to this day.
We follow each other on Instagram.

He DMd me recently asking me if I could buy a shirt for his new business.
I didn't hesitate.
Bought it as soon as I read it.

A couple of years ago, he asked me if I could like his brother's Facebook page for his wedding reception business.
I didn't hesitate.
I liked it immediately.

Ali had my back for plenty of months when I was in Virginia.
Gave me rides, tips on how to succeed in the company and all that.
But I remember him for the fried chicken.

He also showed me that different people show caring in different ways.
I wasn't able to read Ali that well because I was like him myself.

I would rather drop you off at the airport without charging you rather than sitting you down and talk about feelings with you.

Since I was so similar to Ali, I wasn't able to speak his language.
Sometimes, being too similar creates blind spots.

With social skills, different people express themselves differently.
Some do it with words.
Some do it with subtle actions.
Some do it with both.

It's not a game of finding which one is right and which one is
wrong.
It's about finding what language that person is speaking from
their worldview.

By spotting nuances like this, people who seem very angry can
morph into someone who is very caring, instantaneously.

Not in increments.
But instantaneously.

So this is a way to empathize.
By seeing how there is an Ali in your life who gave you fried
chicken....yet, you weren't able to tell.

It's more than the fried chicken.
With people, it's always the intention you want to weigh first.

THE WEASEL

I saw this debate a while back with this very annoying lady.
She looked annoying.

That's bad of me to say.
But let me explain what I mean.

You ever seen a stranger who looked very similar to a person you knew?
The similarity was stunning.

So you stood there.
Waiting to hear this stranger speak.
Did this stranger also SOUND like the person you knew?

Eventually, this person speaks.
And shows their body language.

And you're stunned.

This stranger not only looks like your friend.
But acts like your friend too!

I'm sure you can think of one moment when this happened to you.
How strange, isn't it?

Every now and then I can tell if I'll get along with someone or not.
I won't rely on this too much.
It's just a general feel.
A gut instinct.

Back to the debate that I was watching with the annoying lady.
This woman had a smug look on her face.
Something about her just gave me bad vibes.

As the debate progressed, it seemed like she was debating just to prove why she was right, rather than hearing anyone else's perspective.

Cutting people off, raising her voice & looking like she was planning her comeback when someone else was talking.

This lady had that weasel vibe.
'What is a weasel?'
It's a social character that I will discuss shortly.

Eventually, there was another person in the debate who was losing her cool with this smug lady.
She was trying to present facts to this arrogant woman.

But the arrogant woman was like, *'you have your position and I have mine.'*

That's not a bad thing to say.
However, the **way** she said it seemed shaky.

This seemed like the situation with finding a stranger who looks like your friend.
Where you can expect the moves beforehand...

Even though I don't know this lady at all, I have another hunch.
My hunch is that she's one of those people who apologize incorrectly.

You know those people who apologize with an excuse?
"I'm sorry you felt sad, but here's why I was not in the wrong."

I don't know her.
But hey...
Just a hunch.

The weasel is the social character who thinks being a pain in the ass is funny or pleasant.

Some people like drama.
And a life without any drama can get boring.

The weasel goes past that boring territory to actively try to agitate someone.
And this person is often like, 'I just hate drama.'

Spotting a weasel requires a trained eye.
And a weasel can rarely spot another weasel.

'Who can spot this social character Armani?'
Someone who is chill and relaxed.

You ever met someone like that?
Where you could tell this person could get along with anyone you introduced them to?
That sort of person exemplifies social intelligence.

A weasel leaves clues.

Here are a few clues I've noticed.
One of them I already said.
They apologize with an excuse.

Another one is when they make fun of you to people YOU introduced them to.

'Anything else I should look out for?'
Yes.
Watch out for people who argue for the sake of arguing.

This is a toxic person to be around.
That's the vibe that the smug looking lady gave me.

A lot of social intelligence cannot be proven off the bat.
It requires giving people a chance and not judging too soon.

Other times, advice like 'always listen to the gut' is suggested.

The gut knows.
But is the gut always right?
And don't you need training to learn to listen to the gut?

Always listening to your gut instinct is bad advice in my opinion.
If that was the case, logic wouldn't be a thing.

'So, do I go with the gut or go with logic?'
Depends on judgment.

Judgment is built through trial and error.

Sort of like playing darts.
Even the best darts player does not hit bullseye every time.
However, they are much better than their first time.

The first time they played darts, their aim went completely off board.
The time after that, they hit the board.

As more reps came in, the more they got closer to the red target.
Closer.
And closer.
Closer.

BOOM!
Bullseye.

That's how judgment works.
It's never a full 100/100.

There are times to take a big L to the chin.
And say 'I really did misjudge that person.'

And there are times to take an unexpected W.
'Whoa, I was actually right about that person! I didn't have any evidence either.'

That balance of L and W requires the courage to fail.
Otherwise, judgment can never be built.

Was that lady a weasel?
I can never fully know.
And I can sleep well at night not fully knowing.

CHICKEN SCRATCH

Is it just me or do a lot of smart people have sloppy hand writing?
Maybe I'm the only one who noticed that.

I used to be in a class with 2 kids from Asia.
Sean Wang & Jinhee Byun.

Sean was Chinese.
Jinhee was Korean.

They used to hang out all the time during class and in the
cafeteria.
Many of the other students thought they were brothers.

Jinhee would be furious when most of the other students
confused him for being Chinese rather than Korean.
After the confusion, Jinhee would give an in depth explanation of
the difference between the 2 areas.

Jinhee was a unique fellow because he was much older than all
the other kids in our class.
Where most of the other kids were 13, he was **16**!

I heard about kids having a few months age gap.
But 3 years??
Was this even legal?

I didn't know, nor did I care.
Bottom line was that Jinhee was in our class and would routinely
mess up our curves.

He was so smart that our teacher would often want us to meet his
standards.
He was the top dog in the class until Sean transferred into our
school.

Where Jinhee was loud and bold.
Sean was silent & meek.

Sean wasn't smarter than Jinhee.

Both of them met eye to eye in terms of intellect.

What made both of them stick out was how they had a very
disgusting writing style.
It was almost ineligible!

IT WAS AS THOUGH THEIR HANDS COULD NOT KEEP UP WITH THEIR GIFTED MINDS.

I would wonder, are these 2 really smart?
Or is their hand writing so messy where the teacher got confused
and was like...*fuck it, you got an A.*

No, they were smart.

When they weren't doing hand writing, they would seamlessly
lecture the other students.
It was a live view of the Pareto Principle.
2 students rose up while the other 30 were struggling to catch up.

Messy hand writing has been a creative tool of mine.
It's what allows me to have a new email sent out every single day.

My method of journaling is very different from other forms of
journaling.
I don't believe in strucutre....in the beginning at least.
I am a big fan of chaos.

The least of my worries for idea creation is how neat I am writing.
'Does neat hand writing have a spot in your process at all?'
Yes.
But that's a different kind of journaling.
I call that bullseye journaling.

**Bullseye journaling and Freeflow journaling are night
and day.**

I use bullseye to exercise my concentration.
I use freeflow to exercise my creativity.

With bullseye, I write 1 word over and over again for 30 minutes.
And I make sure that I am mindfully present on each letter.

Obviously, my mind drifts.
However, each time I bring the mind back, the stronger the
concentration muscle gets.

Freeflow method is my **fuck it** method.
I write whatever I write.
And I write like I am the only person in the universe.

This method allows me to have a constant stream of ideas that I
can make emails about, create videos on, and write books about.

Isn't that strange?
It's a night and day difference.

Due to my field of communication skills, I leverage both methods
and try to switch it up.
Not going to talk about my writing schedule in this email.
Just wanted to make you aware that journaling has different
types.

Let's say you go to someone who is sweaty and you're like, *what
have you been doing?*
And the person says, 'playing sports.'

You're next question may be, *what kind of sports?*
And the person in an impatient way says, 'sports.'
Pretty much implying that he told you everything that needed to
be said the first time.

Sports is a broad category.
There is basketball, football, skateboarding etc.
He needs to get more detailed.

If you want to begin journaling, I recommend you start
wondering what it is that you want to improve.

*Concentration, more ideas, better hand writing, stronger
introspection skills...*
Something!
Don't be like the dummy who says 'journaling', like the guy who
says, 'sports.'

With all that being said, if you're a beginner looking to get into journaling, I recommend Free Flow method.
Just write whatever comes to your mind.

Eventually, patterns will present themselves and you'll have a framework that works for you.

If you have any questions, then you're already off to the **wrong** start.

You may be like:
-for how long?
-what do I talk about?
-do I really talk about ANYTHING?

If you have any questions, then you're over thinking.
Let me reiterate: <u>just write about whatever.</u>
That's the Free Flow method.

Chicken scratch may be staring at you.
If you never heard of chicken scratch....
It's slang for sloppy writing.

Don't focus on the writing font too much.
Focus on the ideas that the writing fonts represent.

Jinhee and Sean were too smart for their hands.
Yet, that didn't matter.
The teachers saw their genius and their grades indicated that.

PHYSICS VS METAPHYSICS

A lot of debate nowadays on physics vs metaphysics.

Which topic is more important?

Choosing sides will cause someone to miss the bigger picture.

It's not a matter of if 'what' observations are better suited to explain reality.

Or if 'why' questions are better.

It's about:

-How can we merge both fields?

I made a prediction a while back where I said that within the next 12 years, one of the most in demand positions will be the CSO:

-Chief Storytelling Officer.

Coding was king in 2000s.

Then in 2010, data work became king.

But in the future, the king will be those who can turn the data into useful insights that sparks behavior.

The brilliance of this field is that it merges the physical with the metaphysical.

It merges the what with the why.

Let me give you an example...

Imagine that I give you a bunch of data of Air BnBs in Chicago.

You can find out anything you want to know.

Only problem?
You have 0 desire to ever go to Chicago.

What's the most you can do with that data?
You can be like:
'Well, this Air BnB looks cool.'

Not much useful value is being produced.

Now imagine another scenario where your boss comes into your office and says:

'Hey, I'm taking my wife to Chicago for our honeymoon. My budget is X dollars. I want an Air BnB within walking distance of tourist spots and restaurants.

Now you can look at the data with purpose.
You can provide useful value to the boss and his wife.
Your insights spark behaviors in others.

Data storytelling doesn't stop with Air BnBs.
It begins with Air BnBs and leads to **you**.

View your life experiences as data.
The good, the bad, and the ugly.

The narrative is up to you (hopefully).
Otherwise, a narrative will be assigned (society, mainstream media, politicians etc).

After finding the correct why (purpose), you can process the what (experiences) from a completely new light.

That's when what observations shake hands with why questions.

OPERATING SYSTEM

The computer has 2 types of software.

The operating system software.

The application layer software.

The operating system is for resource management.

It allows for the electricity to efficiently turn off and on.

For the most part, the operating system is invisible to us.

It lies in the background.

The application layer are the stuff that is **real to us.**

It's the Word document, Excel sheet, Google chrome, Twitter app etc.

I view the operating system (OS) of a human as their subconscious mind.

Their storehouse of beliefs.

Imagine an application that was strictly written strictly for Mac OS.

Then you get that application and try to jam it into Windows OS.

Will it run?

Nah.

Because the application program needs to be compatible with the operating system.

Otherwise, it'll reject.

This is why I find it very comical when 2 people are arguing.

Sometimes, arguments are needed.
Sometimes, debates are needed.

However, the question is:
What is the end goal?

Is this person someone you are in charge of?
Sort of like a parent to a son.

Are you getting paid to debate this person?
Where 2 intellectual thinkers are going head to head for compensation?

Or are you just a dude on Facebook who disagrees with someone else's post?
Now you're spending most your Saturday just going back and forth with this other person.

You're trying to install the application program you wrote for Windows OS into the person.
But look closer...
Their operating system is Mac.

So your application (idea) will be rejected.
All you're doing is wasting time.

Focus on something better.
'Like what?'

Like evolving the minds of those who have the same fundamental beliefs.

Y'all are on the same page.

This will save a lot of time.

Now you can use that added time to create stunning applications on the correct operating system.

WHY BOY BANDS BREAK APART

I've always found it strange that boy bands break up at their prime.
They were on top of the world.
They will surely keep the momentum going, no?

Surprisingly, no...
They break up.

And they don't just break up in a civil way.
There is a lot of drama involved.

You can replace 'boy bands' with any collective group that works together for prolonged periods of time.

It seems like when humans are around each other for too long, drama is bound to ensue.

I'll give you a funny story about this.

A while back, I was thinking about joining a fraternity.
Before joining, I remember meeting a cool kid at the recruiting event.
He was the one of the guys who talked me into pledging.

In the beginning of the pledge process, all was going well.
But around the end of the process, all the pledges had to be in 1 house.

During this time of living in 1 house together, that's when I realized the cool guy wasn't that cool.
He was a dirty bastard.

He had this bad habit of putting his hands in food.
He'd stick his index finger straight into the peanut butter jar, lick the peanut butter off his finger, then stick his finger back in the jar!!

Im like:

'Bro, you just use your finger like that? You can't use a spoon?'

He's like:
'What's the problem, man? I washed my hands.'

And I'm like:
'No, you didn't! I literally saw you come back from the gym and stick your dirty ass hand in the peanut butter jar!!!'

If he was acting this liberal with the peanut butter, I wonder what the hell he was doing with the orange juice.

The cool kid suddenly transformed into a very inconsiderate kid in my eyes.

It's like that with a lot of boy bands.
They are in a closed system of a tour bus.
And who knows what sort of quirks each member discovers about each other.

Keep them in the system for too long... that's when tiny issues become gargantuan.
Fights are bound to ensue.

One fix I found for this was to introduce the Friendship/Acquaintance dynamic.
This is when you are half friend, half acquaintance.

Friend, as in you guys spend tons of hours together.
-Maybe due to a joint venture, work project, hosting a show together etc.

But at the same time, there is an acquaintance-like relationship where there are **hard** boundaries up.

2 Types of Boundaries:

- You guys avoid talking about personal lives: Rule-based boundary.
- You guys are capable of collaborating despite living in different countries: Space-based boundary.

I've noticed that groups that fully become friends often implode.
But groups that are pure acquaintances never develop the
chemistry to take it to the next level.

It appears, the hybrid of the 2 is what allows a working
relationship to stand the test of time.

PET PEEVES

A pet peeve is a minor annoyance.
Don't let the word 'minor' fool you.
Minor can turn into major real quick.

I used to know this kid who hated walking on grass.
His whole mood would change if he would step on anything that
wasn't cement.

How peculiar.
What a strange pet peeve to have.

Eventually, I would notice this guy routinely wear white shoes.
His shoes were normally clean and polished.

2 and 2 started to click.
Did he despise the grass because he didn't want to get his shoes
dirty?

Of course!

But no...
That wasn't the case.

There were plenty of times he'd wear raggedy shoes to play
basketball.
Dark shoes at that.
And his disdain for grass was still there.

This was *his* pet peeve.
Noted.

I thought this person was strange.
Who has such a problem with grass?
Oh well, it's his walking path of choice, not mine.

As a few years went by, I ended up working in this company with
a big campus.

One day, when I was walking into work, I noticed a path right by the parking lots that seemed to be calling my name.

I never saw this path before...
I wonder where it leads to?

So I decided to be a few minutes late for work to see where this path headed.
As I followed the trail....I soon became amazed.

It took me to a brand new side of the campus that I never knew existed!

It was a path in nature, that stood over a lake with Koi fish.
This was awesome.

What made it better was that others must not have known about it because only 4 other people would walk there.
I was one of the 4.

Routinely, I would walk in this area with my headphones on.
There was a nice pace I'd walk in which allowed the walks to feel like a breeze.

As a few months started to go on by, more and more people started to discover this path.

What was once empty was now picking up foot traffic.
A bit too much foot traffic for my liking.

My nice paced walks now turned slower and slower.
Rather than simply walking, now I was walking and weaving.

I started to notice a pet peeve of mine.
'What was that?'
Slow walkers walking in front of me.

I hated that.
Couldn't stand it one bit.

People who I normally thought were so cool, turned sour in my perception when I found out they were a slow walker.
The nerve of these people!!

As more time went on by, I noticed different people used the pathway for different intents.

I used it to walk, visualize, burn calories and stay in shape.

Others used it for a different reason.
Plenty of the other walkers had a long day at work, and were using the pathway to unwind.

If you're trying to unwind, then walking slow makes more sense.
They were trying to walk in a pace where they could have a conversation & soak up the scenery.

That's when I realized that I was probably the one being perceived as the kid who hated walking on grass.
The slow walkers probably viewed me to be the weird one!

'Who is this guy walking so fast? Why doesn't he slow down a little? His fast pace is annoying me and giving me anxiety. I'm already having a long day at work!'

Not that I walk fast.
Fast is relative.
A moderately higher than usual walk pace will be seen as rapid to a slow walker.

This whole game of pet peeves just got confusing.
-I found them annoying because they were slow.
-They probably found me annoying because I was fast.

There is a lot of speculation going on in this talk.
Maybe they weren't annoyed.
Maybe they didn't even notice me.

However, it just goes to show the potential of how a minor can be a major in someone else's view point.

1. Spotting your own pet peeves builds self awareness.
2. Spotting someone else's pet peeves builds a deeper understanding of body language.

I had no clue I had a minor annoyance in walk pace until I went through it.
And even after I went through it, I wasn't able to put it into words until years later.

Back then, I'd just get annoyed and react.
Would vilify the slow walkers.

As I write this, I see their perspective.
That's why writing is good...it builds self awareness.

Spotting the pet peeves of others builds fluency in body language.
That's because others are not always comfortable expressing what annoys them.

The kid who hated walking on grass would normally do this grunt when the cement walkways were ending.
He would rarely say 'Geez Armani, I really hate walking on this thing called grass.'

People are rarely clear like that.
Some are.
But clarity is a present surprise.

Pet peeves are a compass to something more.
Yes, the definition says it's a *minor* annoyance.
But the minor can turn into major.
And annoyance can turn into insight.

These are the hidden footprints that can help build social intelligence over time.

To get started, try spotting a few of your pet peeves that you never articulated before.
You may even surprise yourself.

SAM

There was a period in my life when I was a part of 3 different Toastmasters clubs.

2 around the Tampa area & 1 at work.

The first club that I thought about joining was called "Suncoast Toastmasters."

In the club was a man named Sam.

Sam was in his 60s and was Bengali.

He used to be a pilot in his early days and I think he also served in the Navy.

Something like that.

When I walked into the club, he could immediately tell I was Bengali.

Not Indian or Pakistani....But Bengali...

He came up to me and asked, *'Kemon Acho Bhaia?'*

Which means, How are you brother?

I was surprised he knew where I was from.

I responded back, *'bhalo achi, apne kemon achen?'*

Which means, 'I'm doing well, how are you?'

We spoke for a little and he told me to sit next to him.

He was a veteran in the club and could tell that I was a newbie.

Sam was also the former president for this chapter, so he had some clout.

As the meeting progressed, he was whispering why the members were doing what they were doing.

At one point, people would snap their fingers a lot.

When people snap their fingers in a Toastmasters meeting, that's because a member used the *'word of the day'* in their talk.

Each meeting has a new 'word of the day.'

When the speaker's go up on stage, the audience members clap...

Not just a brief clap.

But they clap until the speaker goes from the chair **all the way** to the stage.

If the speaker is a slow walker, then the audience will be clapping for some time.

The members clapped like that to get the speaker hyped up for the talk.

I liked that.

Seemed like everyone was close.

It came to a point when Table topics was coming up.

This was the impromptu speech section of the meeting.

Sam was the first to volunteer and gave an elegant speech about candles.

He seemed like he had been wanting to give that speech his entire life by the way his words just flew out.

Once he was done, I noticed him whisper something to the Table Topics Master's ear.

The Table Topics Master is the person who has all the random topics and chooses members from the audience to participate.

This man's name was Greg.

Once Sam sits down next to me, I said that he did an excellent job.

He looks at me, smirks and says, *'now it's your turn.'*

Soon as he says that, Greg looks my way and says, *'our next speaker will be the guest, Arman!'*

I looked at Sam pissed.

Man...

I don't want to talk in front of all these people. I just came to chill and get a feel for the club.

It was too late.

Greg called me on stage and gave me a pretty deep topic.

It was about what I have to say to Holocaust deniers.

It was a strange talk on my end.

I went through it.

Yet, I did it with my body feeling off.

Heated skin, dry mouth, very nervous.

The 2 minutes felt like 15 minutes.

Once I was done, Sam gently put his hand on my shoulder and said, *'Good job on not being a pussy.'*

This man Sam was some piece work.

His teeth were orange.

In my culture, a lot of Bengali's eat a thing called Paan.

It's this leaf like thing with tobacco which gives you a buzz.

I could tell that Sam loved Paan.

When you eat it a lot, your teeth turns orange.

He was a very blunt guy.

If you are one of those politically correct guys, you'd hate him.

Sam was conservative and would let you know what was on his mind.

For the next couple of weeks, Sam served as a great resource to learn from.

He taught me how to think faster, how to network with other members and also urged me to take up leadership positions in the club.

I liked Sam because he wasn't politically correct.

Didn't waste too much time sugarcoating.

I learned that the hard way in my first ever speech called the 4 haircuts.

This was my Icebreaker.

The first talk you give once you become a member.

Overall, the talk went smooth.

I was a clear 2nd place.

Sam was very harsh on me during the evaluation...

Apparently my back was facing the right side of the audience the entire time.

He gave me very little praise.

Then continued to evaluate me by pointing out my errors. The main error he was caught up on was how my back faced an entire segment of the audience.

I was annoyed because I was thinking, *damn dawg, this is my first speech. If you weren't so harsh, I think I would of won first place!*

I didn't tell him that though.

He knew what he was doing.

After the meeting, he came to me and said, *'great speech.'*

'Great?? You just roasted me' I said in a joking way.

He said he needed to otherwise I'd never learn.

Sam was a tough love kind of person.

His piercing evaluation taught me to never have my back facing a segment of the audience for an entire speech.

Since his evaluation was so harsh, his lesson actually spilled over to my social skills realm as well.

You ever had that moment when you and a group are talking in a circle...

And one dumbass starts facing his back towards you, slowly edging you out of the conversation?

You try getting back in, but this person's back is serving as a wall...

That's what Sam was talking about in terms of public speaking.

Such common sense advice.

Not rocket science.

There are segments of the audience, so respect all sides.

That was just one lesson that I learned from my time in Toastmasters.

I doubt I'd ever learn it until I actually gave a speech.

Doubt there are articles which talk about 'why you shouldn't face your back to the audience.'

Even if public speakers may want to write a post on it, plenty won't because no one is searching for it.

These public speakers may be like, *'why would I write an article on this? It can't even be optimized for Google.'*

That's the unfortunate truth.

A lot of practical accounts fall under the radar because their hyper targeted insights are not questions which are normally asked.

IMPERFECTIONS

During Toastmasters, I learned the concept of over practicing.
Over practicing is not a good thing.
It creates a negative emotion towards the speech.

The speaker subconsciously thinks:
*'Geez I need to practice a **ton**, otherwise, I will fail in front of others.'*

After a certain period of practicing, the speaker gets diminishing returns.
Each rep makes the speaker feel less competent.

That's why I like the 5x rule.
Get through your speech 5 times to **perfection**.
Anytime you fumble (even if it's in the last 10 seconds) start over.

By perfection, I don't mean to recite the words verbatim each time.
I mean to keep the main points and deliver them in a way that you're satisfied with.

Once you pass the 5x rule, the speech is in the subconscious mind.

With writing, there is a concept known as overediting.
Where you're editing your personality away!

Michael Jackson said he was never satisfied with his work.
He said he always found different ways for the songs to be better.

That's how a creative person's mind works.
The next tweak will make it better.

Luckily, Michael Jackson had Quincy Jones and other producers to be like:
'Hey, you're good! We're going with this.'

When you keep editing over and over again...

The main intent of creative writing is lost.

Creative writing is about writing like you talk.
But with each rep you edit, you're getting more and more
polished with the grammar.

That's not bad in doses.
But when you overdo it, that's when the writing sounds robotic.

Instead, the personality should lead the charge!
Mentally re-read your writing and **feel** like you are talking to
you.

Just like we need to know when to stop practicing the speech.
We need to know when to stop editing and hit publish.

With writing, imperfections can be an asset.

ABRUPT CHANGES

Picture something that you are embarrassed of.
Let's say it's public speaking.

You're terrified of speaking with 500 people staring at you.
Gives you the willies.

Now imagine that I say:
'Instead of giving the speech in front of 500 people, you will give the speech in your room.'

How will you feel?
'Not bad at all!'

It's the same speech.
However, due to a change in environment, your emotional state is different.

-Humans are not afraid of failing.
-They are afraid of being **judged** for failing.

But that's not what I'm going to be talking about today.
I'm going to be talking about the remix.

-People are not annoyed of hearing bad news.
-They are annoyed of **not being given updates** prior to the bad news.

The more abrupt and shocking the news, the more you need to give continual updates.

A lot of people just dump the news on the other person rather than give updates because they wrongfully assume that it will lower the likelihood of a confrontation.
But that's not the case.

Humans like it when they are informed.
It's allows them to accept the bad news quicker.

If you're a contractor who tells your client that you need 4 extra weeks to complete the job **on delivery date**, they will be pissed!

But if you're a contractor who begins giving updates **prior to the delivery date**, something strange happens.

By week 1, the client is upset for the delayed deadline.
But by week 2, they processed their feelings.

Keep giving the updates in a gentle way....

By week 3, the client feels like you and them are solving the conflict together.
(When I say solving the conflict together, I mean figuratively, not literally. Don't give the client a hammer and ask them to pitch in lol).

The main difference between a friend and an acquaintance is:
-With a friend, we go through the ups and downs with them.
-While with an acquaintance, going through the ups and downs with them is not needed.

So, when you missed the deadline, you and the client went through a down together.
As long as you give continual updates and finish the job with flying colors... you guys are entering an up together!
The up & down friend loop is activated.

Once the 4 weeks are up, they have a stronger affinity for you.

This isn't always the case.
But it's a strange dynamic in many complex projects.
Where a missed deadline handled appropriately can strengthen the bond, rather than deteroriate it.

The more abrupt and shocking the news.
The more communication that is needed.

Now the likelihood of bad blood plummets.

PAPERBACK

Last year, it was bought to my attention that people listen to audiobooks.
I knew audiobooks were a thing before...
But I thought it was something people hadn't really incorporated into their lives.

Last year, I was part of a business networking club in Tampa.
In this club, each member gives a featured presentation every week.

For my week of presenting, I decided to do a talk on my first book, Level Up Mentality.
I gave its origin story and a little overview of what to expect in the chapters.

After my talk, 4-5 people went on Amazon and purchased a paperback copy.
1 purchased the Kindle version.

And a handful of people asked if there was an audio version.

An audio version?
Hm...
No, I don't have an audio version.

A few of these people went onto tell me WHEN and HOW they consume books.

In this networking group, we were required to have at least two 1 on 1 meetings with a few of the members every week.
This was a lovely feature that allowed the group to function well.

I ended up having a 1 on 1 with one of the guys who asked me if I had an audio book.

He went onto tell me that reading the text in a paperback book hurts his eyes.
Also, he drives a lot.

So when he drives, he normally just plays an audio book on his ride.

What I'm saying may sound like common sense.
But for a person who normally reads paperbacks or a kindle, it's as though my **worldview opened up.**

Especially considering I write books.
This should have been basic knowledge.
But it wasn't.

Information technology does play a role on communication & communication plays a role on information technology.

I wrote a tweet yesterday that said the more that technology advances, the more communication skills will be required.
Don't think most people understood what it meant.

It basically meant that busy work will become automated work.
Tasks that required a lot of elbow grease in the past can easily be taken by a PowerShell script.

Even with coding.
A lot of coding nowadays comes down to connecting puzzles, rather than writing things completely from scratch.

With technology making things more automated, plenty of people are left scratching their heads asking:
'Well, what do I do?'

I went to a Chase bank recently to pick up some quarters.
And when I went in, the employees looked bored as fuck.

Soon as I stepped through the doors, 2 of them jumped my way and asked what they could help me with...
As if they needed something to do.

I told the 2 ladies that I needed quarters.
That's when their eyes lit up.

Most of the tasks that day were probably being done through the machines.

If you don't have a Chase bank around your area, then just know they have invested a ton of money into their technology sector.

Stuff like withdrawing money is something that can easily be done by a machine.
Not much human intervention needed.

This is just one field where technology made it easier on the employee's life.
However, imagine if a district manager or someone like that walked in.

Looking at the bored employees .
Just chilling and waiting for something to do.
The first thought the district manager may have will be, 'wait, why do I have so many people working in this branch?'

So communication and technology are intertwined.
What sparks fear in some sparks joy in others.

The fearful people are like:
 'gee willekerz....what if a machine takes my job?'

The joyous people are like:
'these machines make other facets of my life so much easier.
Now I can do creative tasks!'

One of the reasons I was very surprised about the fact that people consume audiobooks was because audiobooks were not even a thing when I was growing up.

It was paperback.

Nowadays, with the advancement of technology, it gives people with long commutes a chance to turn their car into a learning station.

The title of this talk was paperback...
That's because no matter how advanced technology gets, the actual feel of the book is what always gets me.

It's good in my opinion to have some preferences for things as technology rises.

Otherwise, all technology looks like something that we HAVE to incorporate into our lives.

With some preferences of our own, it's easier to respect someone else's taste without finding the need to make it a part of our life.

The people who asked me for an audiobook may view the paperback as a dinosaur method.
It's good that they have their preferences too.

Technology strikes fear in some.
Technology strikes joy in some.

Either way, technology & communication are intertwining.

KEVIN SAMUELS

I saw this man named Kevin Samuels on YouTube plenty of years ago.
He was a skinny man with great fashion sense.

One of his videos popped up when I was looking for certain cologne suggestions.
I watched the video, got some advice & went about my day.

I found out that he had been blowing up on YouTube as of late.
But nowadays, he did not mainly cover fashion.
He covers dating & marriage in his content.

I heard about his show blowing up when there was a girl I knew from Tampa who called into his show.

One of my friends messaged me on WhatsApp and was like, *'hey, are you watching Kevin Samuels live right now?? Sarah is on it!'*

I forgot who Sarah was.
I think she went to my college?
And I forgot who Kevin Samuels was.

So this contact sent me the link & enthusiastically was like, *'go check it out! The show is live.'*

As I watched the show, I recognized who Sarah was.
But more importantly, I recognized who Kevin was.

Wait a minute!
He was the cologne guy.
I didn't know that was his name. What a small world.

As I watched his show, I noticed him consistently use a phrase:
-High Value Man.

For some of you, that phrase registers something in your mind.
For some of you, that phrase does not register anything in your mind.

What I noticed him doing was creating a phrase or popularizing it.

I'm sure high value man was used a lot before.
And it means different things to different people.

But for Kevin's viewers, the phrase meant something **targeted**.

There are a few requirements he has for the phrase of high value man:
Making 5 figures a month, strong network, effective digital footprint, physically fit etc.

But he didn't keep listing out the descriptions that I listed in the line above.
He simply said 'high value man' and it created a short circuit in the caller's mind.

He'd ask 'are you looking for a high value man' to the caller who called in.
And from there, she would respond with yes or no.

This is how words build over time.
It's a look into the mind & evolution of perception.

When I first started tweeting in 2018, I'd routinely use the phrase, tityboy.

Tityboy was my way of poking some fun.
And jabbing victim mentality.

This got a lot of laughs.
And made the message heard.

Tittyboy is not a phrase in the dictionary.
It's just an imaginary phrase used in an ambiguous context to short circuit the mind.

I came to find out later on that popular rapper 2 Chainz, rap name used to be Tityboi.
Same pronunciation.
Different spelling.

But if he was called that phrase, I doubt he'd view it in a comical fashion.
He'd view it in a serious fashion.

Why?
Because prior to 2 Chainz, Tityboi represented his career.

Kevin Samuels use of High Value Man & my use of tityboy have a lot in common.
And that's called short circuiting.

All words develop like that by the way.
There is a common pattern or a desire to express a common pattern.
Then utterances & play on words from pre-existing words are twisted & morphed.

When I was in the 7th grade, I visited Bangladesh.
And a few of my aunts came to me and were like:
'Armani, I hear you kids call girls chicks over there. Is this true?

I proudly nodded my head.

'But chicks are baby chickens. Why would you call women that?'
I looked at them confused.
You all don't do that here?

We don't mean actual chicks.
The other 7th graders used it as slang.

I can keep going on with this.
What about 'get the bag.'

Get the bag implies getting the money.
Yet, it implies more than getting the money.
It can eventually be warped into a lifestyle.

I saw this podcast not too long ago where 2 of the hosts were encouraging this upcoming model to start an Only Fans.

She refused.

But they kept telling her to start one.

Once again, she refused and talked about the stigma around Only
Fans.
Her argument was that she didn't want that stigma around her.

But the hosts argument was:
'Get the bag.'
They kept reiterating that phrase.
It was more than a phrase for them.
It was a philosophy.

'What does all this imply Armani?'
What this implies is that it's not too difficult to get someone to
think a certain way.

Which is why I encourage self knowledge.
Asking deep questions like who am I ?

And looking beyond surface level answers like reciting your name
like a parrot.
Or saying what you do for a living.

Go deep into the question.

And that's when it leads to:
*is consciousness fundamental or does consciousness come from
the brain?*
That's the question that the deep thinkers are led to.

'That question comes from asking who am I?
It certainly does.
Over time, of course.

Questions are deep & reveals true insight.
Thru true insights, it's easier to play YOUR game.

Words are scoffed at.
But words can be structured in a way to alter someone's behavior.

Good or bad.
Up or down.

Remember that, my friend.
Always keep that in mind.

DANE COOK

In 2006 ish, Dane Cook was on fire.
He was clearly one of the top comics out there.

At first, I thought he did too much.
As if he was too animated with his delivery.
Later, he grew on me.

I liked how he had passion and a lot of energy.
If I was having a bad day, watching him would create a flurry of positive energy in the environment.

I think I was in 11th grade when he was on fire.
The other kids liked him as well.
They would repeat his jokes and try to deliver it the same way he did.

As a few months went by, Dane Cook became even more on fire!
He made an elegant transition from comedy to movies.

What can this guy NOT do??

As a couple of years passed by, something began to change.
'What?'
People slowly began turning on Dane Cook.

Earlier, if I said Dane Cook was funny, others would be like:
'Duh! What was your favorite comedy special?'

Nowadays, if I said he was funny, they'd be like:
'Bro, he sucks! Let me tell you why.'

Eventually, I was outnumbered.
If I said I found Dane funny, the entire group would turn on me.

Hm... that's strange.
Just a few years earlier, he was on fire.
Why was the tide shifting?

It wasn't only the consumers who were turning on him.
Plenty of his peers began talking shit about him too.

There were comedians who said he bit their jokes.
Late night talk show hosts clowned him.
And Joan Rivers referred to him as an asshole.

Suddenly, Dane Cook disappeared.
It's like he fell off the face of the planet.

A parallel to this was T-Pain in the hip hop industry.
In 2006ish, T-Pain was on fire, had mainstream success & could do no wrong.

Then autotune (the staple of T-Pain's music) became 'uncool.'
Just like that...T-Pain's meteoric success was followed by a meteoric plummet.

Luckily, in this era, it's easier than ever to get your message out there.

Dane Cook has been one of the people sharing his past in recent interviews.

When an interviewer asked why others hated him soooo much, he answered that question in 2 parts.

For the 1st part, he said that he wasn't completely hated.

Considering that he had 20,000 people in the audience coming to watch him perform.

After acknowledging his admirers, for the 2nd part, he dissected the hate he received.

When asked why he was so hated, he simply said:

'I don't know.'

Sure, there were some behaviors he did back then that makes his modern self cringe.

He said one of his regrets was that he dressed very douchey back in the days.

But on the big picture level, Dane said his intentions weren't bad.

He just wanted to make people laugh.

Why the vitriol against him?

There may be a few things he did that were sinister that I am completely unaware of...however, my hypothesis is 2 fold:

1. People often turn and then come back in the long run.

2. When the masses see a majority of people turning on someone, they just follow the herd.

Dane had so much success that it was inevitable that the balloon was going to pop.

There is the famous quote:

'They build you up to tear you down.'

I've noticed that in the long run, a lot of these people who were savagely taken down are revisited again in the future with admiring lens.

Recently, Britney Spears serves as a modern example of that.

She was a superstar in the late 90s & early 2000s.

Then around 2006ish, she became the international punching bag.

As over a decade has passed, nowadays, she has a documentary that portrays her as a legendary figure who was unjustly treated.

'Why does this all matter to me? I'm not trying to become a celebrity.'

Even if you're not trying to become a celebrity (which I think is an awful goal to set) I think it's smart to be aware of the media landscape in general.

It's been estimated that the average person consumes 7 hours of media (tweets, books, blogs, YouTube videos) a day.

7 hours!! That's staggering!!!!

Plus, in this era, more people than ever are doing **some** form of content creation online.

I found out lately that one of my client's mom creates memes for her WhatsApp chat.

I asked him why she does that.

He said:

'Because my mom is known as the funny auntie in her friend group. So she makes funny memes of trending topics to get more laughs and bond with the group.'

That's a form of content creation.

With a solid grasp of the media landscape from the past and present, it becomes much easier to focus on the fundamentals and not personalize trends.

It's sort of like an investor who reads everything.

They don't just read books on investing.

They read books on metaphysics, history, finance and more.

This allows them to develop a bird's eye view of the subject rather than being susceptible to what's hot right now.

They become like a tree that does not easily waver.

This allows them to stick to their plan no matter how windy the environment is!

With new media, it's difficult to see who will have another shot at success.

T-Pain, who fell off the face of the planet is nowadays making a stunning resurgence with his Twitch channel.

Also, in this era, he is viewed as a legend who was ahead of his time!

Try listening to modern hip hop without some form of autotune.

With a longer focal point of the media landscape, it becomes easier to carry your brand with authenticity, integrity, and value.

Haters come and go.

As do trends.

But the legendary ones stay, no matter how the tides shift.

IT'S THE PIZZA, STUPID

Identity is important with content creation.

It's the underlying theme that influences every word.

Highly important and allows the creator to focus.

From intense focus, creativity is born.

Allow us to leave the world of content creation to enter the world of Pizza real quick.

'Pizza??'

Yes, more specifically, Papa John's Pizza.

The founder of the Papa John's pizza empire is John Schnatter.

He started the company in a broom closet.

After months of tinkering, he was able to create a pizza that was enjoyed by others.

He knew his calling was to be a pizza maker.

There was problem.

Or better yet...

Problems.

Dominoes and Pizza Hut.

Those were the 2 big dogs in the Pizza market.

Was John dreaming too big to think he could take them on?

Dominoes had speed on their side.

While Pizza Hut had brand recognition.
How would Papa John's stick out?

After thinking for some time...
It clicked!

Better ingredients.

John used quality ingredients in making his pizza, and that was the main differentiator.

He wanted Papa John's to have a mom and pop feel no matter how big the chain got.

For the next couple of years, Papa John's expanded from John's broom closet to building franchises all over the US.

When the company went public, John became worth 100 million dollars overnight.

Things were looking great.
Now it was off to the stars!!

Until...
'Until what?'
Until early 2000s happened.

Papa John's had grown so rapidly that it bought unexpected problems.

And one of the problems was lower quality pizza.

The crusts were hard.
There were not enough cheese.
And each pizza from each restaurant looked different.

To make matters worse, the franchisees started to get cute.

They wanted to add wings, toys, and merchandising to the Papa John's stores.

John was mortified.

His life's work was to ensure that his pizza's had quality.

Nowadays, his pizzas were junk!

For the next **4 years**, he did his best to bring quality back to the Papa John's empire.

But each time, he ran into roadblocks.

His empire had grown so big that it felt like everyone spoke different languages.

He didn't know what to do.

One day, he had an idea.

The company that supplied Papa John's with the pizza sauce was apparently led by a genius businessman.

John contacted this businessman to see if he could give some suggestions on how to bring back quality to Papa Johns.

This businessman agreed to the meeting.

The 2 sat down looking at each other.

The businessman looked John in the eyes and said:

'It's the pizza, stupid.'

John had a stunning realization.

The businessman followed it up with…

'Nowadays, when I got to a Papa John's restaurant, it feels like a chain restaurant. I don't get that same mom and pop feel anymore. What changed?'

John said:

'We lost focus of our mantra.'

'Which was?' the businessman said.

'Better ingredients. Better pizza. Papa John's.'

That was the identity!!!

When John got crystal clear on that, he had a battle cry that everyone could rally around.

They were on the road to speaking the same language again.

They weren't a wings company, or a toy company, or a cookies company.

They were a pizza company first.

Every move they would make would be to complement the pizza.

The pizza was the king and everything else was a royal servant.

What is your battle cry?

That **one line** that encompasses the entire company?

For ArmaniTalks, it's:

Confidence through Communication.

And those words can be further subdivided if need be.

Confidence means clarity.

Clarity means enhanced perception.

And communication is subdivided into the 5-6 mighty soft skills:

1. Level Up Mentality (concentration).
2. Emotional Intelligence.
3. Creativity.
4. Storytelling.
5. Public speaking.
6. Social skills.

All content I create with the ArmaniTalks brand falls under the umbrella of Confidence through Communication.

This allows me to be consistent without ever facing writer's block.

Creativity and rules are not enemies.

As a matter of fact, rules allow someone to be more creative!!

Without a semblance of rules, you have anxiety in the making.

That's why a lot of creative people go insane.

By having some rules (I like to call them non-negotiables) it makes it easier to avoid information overload.

Little to no information overload = Better decision making & effortless creation.

It took Papa John's himself 4 years to realize it was always about the pizza.

And from that, he was able to bring the company back on track.

What is your battle cry?

The one mantra that rules them all...

AMAZING

'How do I improve my communication skills?'
What are your ideas?
'Uh...'
Start there.

I learned a lesson the hard way a couple of years back. The lesson dealt with the difference between the 'what' and the 'how' mentality.

For a while, whenever I was networking with other people who did some public speaking in their days, I'd ask them 'how' questions.

How do I stand?
How do I look?
How do I talk?

They would look at me puzzled and with humor at the same time.
'This 20 year old kid is definitely new.'

They would correct my line of thinking.
Focus on the 'what' and the 'how' will take care of itself.

I thought these people were smoking that good weed and drinking that good henny.
Communication was only about the how!

What they were implying was to understand your ideas.

Then you'll build a natural conviction towards expressing yourself.

Now whenever you talk, you are speaking your facts.

You aren't convincing the people that the sky is blue.

You know that the sky is blue from your lens.

It's like you're just stating the obvious.

The tone, posture, and look will morph around the idea.

That's what I got from those speakers insights..

As I worked more on my writing and speaking skills, I came to realize the practical aspects of *curiosity* in regards to communication.

Ideas can be formed through conscious effort or through subconscious play.

Both work.

But one is effort while the other is soothing.

Conscious effort requires a lot of intellectual faculties.

Subconscious play allows the creative side to lead the charge.

I believe everyone has different personalities.

So it's difficult to be like, *'do this, this and this, to be more curious.'*

It's more about looking in the mirror.

I have this wonderful laptop background of a boy from his room looking into the universe.

All he sees are clouds, stars, and planets.

When I look at that image, all writer's block is instantaneously killed.

Not that I get writer's block too much nowadays. You'll see why shortly.

This wallpaper image opens up *my curiosity* regarding the bigger questions of life.

That's when better ideas are capable of being unlocked on my end.

This helps me with the 'what' that these speakers were talking about....

To add onto this, I have been working on a few short story collections recently. 101 short stories, essays and insights to improve communication skills.

As I was in the process of compiling it, I came to notice that I have written **a lot** in the past 2-3 years.

I think it's much more than I initially assumed.

No wonder I don't get writer's block anymore.

As I looked at these short stories, I noticed a stunning resemblance with my laptop background!

Each story looked like a small planet.

The letters in the story looked like tiny people.

One book collection, which has 101 stories, was the galaxy.

-Zooming in and seeing the letters gave me the microscopic view.

-Zooming out and seeing the entire books gave me
the macroscopic view.

The stories looked like tiny people, stars, clouds and galaxies from the laptop image.

That's when I started to think, wait a minute.

What if there is something like this going on in a grander scale?

-What if we are a letter in a story collection?

-What if we are the story collection?

-Is the world from a grand scope of reality just one short story collection??

-Who the hell is the storyteller?!

These ideas were fun, sure.

But it was more than fun...

It served as practical utility for me.

There's good dwelling.

There's bad dwelling.

Which one do you want to hear about first?

'Let me hear the bad first.'

Bad dwelling is when you worry about 'what if' scenarios, regrets and upcoming failures to be.

Sad truth is that the mind naturally tilts this way.

Good dwelling is when you allow the cement to dry.

'Huh??'

Yes, when you let the cement dry.

This is when you ponder on the stuff that you read, the videos that you watched, and the content that you, yourself, created.

Dwelling on meaningful knowledge fires and wires new neural pathways in your brain, allowing for a physiological change.

Dwelling is a skillset that a mega mind should learn to adopt.

Just the good kind of dwelling.

By pondering on these big questions, and having an imaginative mind, that's when the 'what' mentality becomes easier.

Often, in communication, a lot of the 'how' questions are asked due to fear.

And a lot of the fear is born through wanting others to like them.

I'm not speaking for everyone, but I knew when I was asking all the 'how' questions...

A part of that was because I was curious.

A bigger part was because I was fearful.

After those speakers told me to focus on the idea, that's when I was able to put myself in the passenger seat rather than the driver seat.

By putting myself in the passenger seat, I had a clearer vision on how to guide whoever was in the driver seat.

All for me to realize that I was both the driver and the passenger...

It's as though to become a better writer and speaker, you have to know how to wear different hats.

Sometimes, you wear those hats at separate times.

Other times, together.

My laptop background with the boy looking to the universe may not resonate with you.

Heck, it may flat out seem ridiculous.

But this image has allowed me to produce 1000s of stories, generate revenue for my business, connect with readers, get clients etc.

All because it stretched my mind.

You may want to start looking for something that makes you feel small in the grand scheme of things.

That allows the mind to wander.

Not wander in memory lane replaying back mistakes.

Instead, wandering towards, the light, the skies, and the stars that the limited perception can gain access too.

Start off light.

Find the wallpaper.

Find the 'what.'

The 'how' will simply be the byproduct of your seriousness regarding the 'what.'

That's amazing.

ULTERIOR MOTIVES

One of the loneliest positions out there is the entrepreneur
position.
Because the entrepreneur is always dealing with uncertainty.

Very few understand the state of uncertainty.
This is why well-meaning people have little idea what questions
to ask this entrepreneur.

**When an entrepreneur meets another entrepreneur,
they speak the speak the same language.**

It doesn't matter if one person is in lawn care, and the other
person is in the book publishing business.
They know each other.

What I noticed is that a few entrepreneurs get comfortable
enough to sell their services to their entrepreneur friend.

Sometimes, this can go very well.
Other times, it can fail **spectacularly**.

There was this one entrepreneur who helped me out a lot in 2019.
I considered him a friend.
But it got to a point in 2020, where he kept pitching me his
services.

Routinely, he wanted to have a Skype call and talk about which
services I could benefit from.
I blatantly told him I wasn't interested.
Did him one better and gave him referrals of people who were
interested.

But he had his salesmanship hat on.
A lot of salesmen are taught:
*'No doesn't mean no. Just keep asking in different ways until
you get a yes.*

I have a lot of respect for salesmen.
Do what you're taught to do.

But do it on warm leads, not leads who are cold as shit!

Eventually, these techniques got annoying.
I hate when a salesman thinks the person they are selling to is an idiot.

A lot of mystery writers are taught:
-**Never view your readers as stupid.**

The readers are very smart.
They are solving the case with you.
To really surprise them, view your reader as a borderline genius, then write the story.

There came a point where I stopped talking to this dude.
Because I could see where each question was leading.

We were no longer entrepreneur friends.

Months went by....
One day, he hit me up and asked how I was.
I said I was good.
He asked for a quick Skype call.

The first 24 minutes of the call went great.
But the last 7 minutes, I noticed what he was doing.
He was doing another salesmanship technique which was building rapport, then going for the ask **again**.

Nowadays, I just ignore this person.
I've seen the ulterior motives too many times.

Sad thing is I still speak his language.
He initially began to sell his friends when business wasn't going well.
It started around Covid.

A LOT OF ULTERIOR MOTIVES ARE NOT BORN FROM ILL INTENT.

RATHER, IT'S BORN FROM TOUGH TIMES.

Still...from my experience, it's best to set yourself up in a way where you don't try to get friends and family involved in professional transactions (unless they want to).

Asking for help is one thing.
But we wary of selling them, especially if their will is against it.

This doesn't only apply to business.
It's a concept that happens with human dynamics in general.
Selling doesn't always need a product/service.

Selling can happen through:
-Getting someone to adopt the same lifestyle choices as you.
-Asking for a ride.
-Asking for a date.
Etc.

People get too lost in salesmanship.
They lose sight of the person and get caught up in the processes.
They understand the content, no denying that.
But the context is lost.

COPPERFIELD

A few years back, I went to Vegas.
The people I went to Vegas with each had 1 day where they were
in charge of an event.

The day that I was charge, I was going to take the group to David
Copperfield's magic show.

I eagerly booked the tickets.
And I eagerly awaited for everything to go smoothly.

But a few days before the trip, news broke.
Copperfield was being accused of sexual misconduct.
This was possibly going to cancel his events.

I quickly looked for a replacement event.
But everything was either sold out or someone else from the
group already booked it.
I didn't know what to do.

2 days before my day, Copperfield's show was back on.
He was going to perform as expected.

I kid you not...
His event **exceeded** expectations.

Copperfield makes the audience members put their phones in a
compartment before he begins his show.
Which is a bummer because he had so many Snapchat worthy
moments.

2 moments stuck out.

The 1st moment was when he made a car disappear from the
stage.
Which doesn't seem like much.
Especially from a professional magician.

But what made that memory stick out was how he made the car
disappear from stage and float right in front of my face!!

He turned off the lights before he made the car float.
Once the lights turned on, I was **shocked** to see a MASSIVE car, upside, 18 inches away from my face.

There were no strings holding the car up.
Just a vehicle suspended in the air.

'How was the car so close to my face and I didn't even notice a breeze?'

The 2nd part that stood out was how he chose a person from my crew to be a part of his act.

The guy chosen was a skeptical person.
He thought Copperfield was full of shit.
So he was definitely going to try and pull a fast one on Copperfield.

I can't recall the exact magic trick.
But I do recall the skeptical person walking back in defeat after the trick, with the face of:
'How did he do that?'

After the trip, I did some research on Copperfield.
Was he the Harry Houdini of our time?

I discovered his net worth was a staggering 500 million.
That's way more than I was expecting.

A few days ago, I checked again...
This time, he was a billionaire.

Copperfield quietly became a billionaire while incrementally getting great at 1 thing.

"Getting great at 1 thing" is a misleading phrase.
It makes the mind think:
'What's so difficult about that?'

But getting great at 1 thing is difficult indeed.
Because there are layers involved.

For example:
-Magic.
What other layers make up magic?

You only pull a rabbit out the hat and call it a day, no?
No.

I'm sure in the beginning of Copperfield's magic career, he
needed *people* to watch him pull a rabbit out the hat.
So, he had to learn some basic marketing and selling.

Once people came, he had to actually pull the rabbit out the hat.
Which meant that he needed to be competent.

Not only that...
But people didn't just want to see a rabbit being pulled out the
hat.

They wanted to participate with the magician.
The audience members wanted the thrill of having one of them
sawed in half.

-Now David had to get great at psychology and communication
skills.

-He needed to work on his tonality to build suspense during his
magic shows.

-He had to work on his observation skills to see which tricks
inspired awe and which tricks were meh.

You get my point.
The process of getting great at 1 thing allowed Copperfield to
become great at multiple things!

As Swami Vivekananda once said:

**"Take up one idea. Make that one idea your life — think
of it, dream of it, live on that idea. Let the brain,
muscles, nerves, every part of your body, be full of that
idea, and just leave every other idea alone. This is the
way to success."**

THE WRONG MINDSET FOR A RELATIONSHIP

Two incomplete people getting into a relationship to complete each other, ends poorly.

Two complete people getting into a relationship to amplify each other, goes more smoothly.

'Can you explain the difference between incomplete & complete?' Sure. It all begins with one of life's funnier ironies...

-IN ORDER TO BE HAPPY IN A RELATIONSHIP, YOU MUST BE HAPPY ALONE.

'Really?? I am sad now, so I wanted to get into a relationship to become happy.'

Won't work.

'What will happen?'

You will be happy in the initial stages of the relationship. But as time passes, you'll go back to being sad. PLUS, your sadness will spillover & make your partner sad.

Remember, energy is contagious.

'Ah I see...'

Here's the bottom line, you need to become happy alone.

'But what does that really mean?'

The incomplete ones get happiness from their external world. So, they are dependent humans.

The complete ones get happiness from their internal world. So, they are independent humans.

'Okay don't tell anyone, but I fall in the dependent category. Any ideas to fix this?'

Ya, value yourself.

'How?'

By doing something worth valuing. Right now, you are incomplete because you have low confidence.

Spend some time building yourself up. Find a few challenges & overcome them. The more challenges you conquer, the more value you create for yourself.

Added value increases self-esteem which leads to independence.

Now when you are going into a relationship, you bring value to the table. You are no longer someone that somebody has to coddle & baby around.

'Ah I see!'

Remember one major concept..

You are supposed to ENHANCE one another in a relationship. Not fix one another.

Do not think that getting into a relationship with a high value person will magically make all your problems go away.

Only you are responsible for your internal world.

'That makes a lot more sense! Time for me to become an adult &
work on my independence!'

Excellent. Once you feel comfortable alone, you will now feel
more fulfilled in a relationship.

OVERDOSE

'Your aunt is in the hospital' my mom said.

Is she going to make it?

'No clue.'

Damn..

How the hell could this happen?

We literally saw her yesterday.

She seemed off, but not this bad.

We all paced back and forth in our house awaiting the news.

Please do not let her die.

She is such a sweet woman.

Just give her one more chance.

FLASHBACK

Road trip time.

My family and I were going on a trip to Key West.

We rented a huge RV.

The RV had my mom, dad, brother, cousins, uncles, aunties.

'Wow, that is a lot of people!'

Yup, when Bengali's do road trips, we do it big.

'Why were you guys going to Key West?'

Great question.

My uncle & aunt had this huge beach house in Key West.

Our family would go every now and then to unwind, do a barbeque, get on the speedboat, and just bond.

The Key West trips were a few of the greatest memories from my childhood.

Nothing like a fun family reunion to take a break from our busy lives.

PULL UP TO THE DRIVEWAY

Well, we were finally here!

4 hours later, and the RV was finally parked.

My uncle & aunt greeted us with welcoming arms.

They gave us refreshments and took us to the backyard to get the bbq started.

The house was so big.

8 bedrooms & 8 bathrooms.

I am not joking when I said the house was huge.

But I always found something a little weird.

'What?'

Why have such a big house for just 2 people?

'Your uncle & aunt didn't have kids?'

No, they did not. And that is why I was curious why they had such a big house.

Oh well, I am not going to complain.

This place was paradise.

FUN ZONE

My dad & a few of the other uncles got the BBQ started.

My mom & a few of the other aunties were getting the other entrees & side dishes ready.

The kids? We were getting ready to light up that speedboat.

My oldest cousin knew how to drive that thing, so us youngbloods could just sit on our ass and enjoy the view.

That speedboat was honestly the best part of the trip.

Once we got on that, it just felt like we exited reality & entered a new world.

Cruising on the sea, seeing other speedboats, seeing dolphins splashing out of the water, that's what I call paradise.

The trip was going smoothly just like I imagined.
We were on our boat trip for 1 hour until we came back to devour the food.

The adults already had our plates ready to go.

Such positive vibes.
But....

'But what?'

There was someone who did not seem to be participating in the positive vibes.

SOMETHING ON YOUR MIND?

My aunt who lived in the Key West house was very quiet.

Let's call her Kholon aunt.

(In the Bengali culture, we say the name first and then follow it up with aunt. Counterintuitive to the western culture where you say aunt and the name.)

But Kholon aunt was very quiet and isolated from everyone else.

She kept going into the kitchen and sitting down staring idly off into space.

It felt a little spooky, to be honest.

I went up to my mom.

Mom, what's up with Kholon aunt? How come she is just chilling off in the corner?

'No clue son. We asked her if anything was wrong, but she said no. Let's let her do our own thing for a few.'

Hm.. very strange but okay.

I took one more glance and went back to chill with my squad.

Until...

EAVESDROPPING LIKE AN OG

As I was walking back to the rest of my cousins, I heard the uncles overtalking.

They were talking about my aunt.

So your boy hid behind a tree and perked his ear out to hear what was up. I was a little worried.

'Toby, what is wrong with your wife? How come she is by herself?' asked my dad.

(Toby is the fictional name for my uncle.)

'Keep it a secret. But she has been feeling lonely lately. I just opened up a new medical practice and I have been working like a dog' said Toby uncle.

'Okay, you sure everything is okay though? Like is she doing fine, mentally?' asked my dad.

'She said yes. Anyways, let's talk about something else' Toby uncle said.

I could not see anyone since I was behind the tree. But you could tell my uncle was getting a little annoyed with all the questions. He probably was being asked questions about his wife all day.

Hm..

Maybe we are all just overreacting.

I mean we all have bad days, right?

Let's just let her be and focus on having fun.

'Hey Arman, come get schooled in darts homie!' yelled my brother.

Coming!

And I ran off to play some darts.

TRIP BACK

8 hours at Key West, and all the adults finally decided it was enough. Time to head back home.

The trip was a blast!

Probably the best Key West trip so far.

Once we drove back, most of the kids were tired af. They immediately knocked out.

But I stayed up. So did the adults.

The adults did not know I was up though.

EAVESDROPPING LIKE AN OG PART 11

'Anyone else notice what was up with Kholon?' asked one of my aunties.

'Yea, she seems like she is lonely. She seems depressed. I think it would be best if you ladies follow up with her. Maybe there is something going on with her that she does not feel comfortable telling Toby' said one of my uncles.

The ladies in the group all agreed.

They all said they will follow up with her later this week.

They talked a bit more about the Key West trip, and the car went quiet.

Everyone was so tired.

Time to go back to reality.

BACK TO THE PRESENT

More and more of my relatives were coming to our house.

My parents were organizing a prayer to pray for my aunt.

This was so fucking peculiar.

My aunt was such a sweet lady in all of our past trips.

How could she ...

How could she possibly attempt to overdose on pills?

'What??? She tried to commit suicide??'

Yes.

Kholon auntie attempted suicide.

OVERDOSE

We had just taken the trip the day before.

We knew that she was upset, but did not think it was this bad.

But at 7 pm today, Toby uncle called my dad to deliver the news.

Kholon aunt took a massive amount of pills while my uncle was
at work.

This was no sort of mistake.

She clearly knew that she wanted to take her life.

NOW WE WAIT

Every single person in the house was walking back and forth frantically after the prayer.

Many of the women and children were crying & begging God to not let my aunt die.

You could tell the men in the house wanted to cry as well, but they were doing their best to stay strong.

Everyone had their cellphones handy in case ANY news were to be broken.

But at this point, we could not do much.

All we could do was wait.

She was in the Emergency room.

This felt like a nightmare.

But it was not.

It was 100% reality.

RING RING

My dad's phone began to ring.

The crying immediately seized.

It was Toby Uncle calling.

'Shhh.... everyone quiet' my dad said.

My dad picked up.

'Toby, is everything okay? We are all praying and so worried.'

My dad then stopped.

I could hear chatter from my uncle.

My dad listened.

And listened.

And listened.

And then the chatter stopped.

My dad opened his mouth to respond.

'I am so sorry for your loss Toby, I am so sorry.'

My auntie was announced dead.

ISN'T IT SAD?

I still think about my lost aunt so much.

I loved her.

She was one of the first aunties who would genuinely ask about my hobbies.

She was such a caring, sweet, humble woman.

But she is no more.

Isn't it sad?

Someone can look fine from the outside & be shattered internally?

Isn't it sad?

That someone feels so crippled internally that they cannot even seek help.

Isn't is sad?

That sometimes a bad day is actually more than just a 'bad day'?

Ya.

It's sad.

I miss you Kholon aunt.

Sorry that you suffered in silence.

WHAT I WANT YOU TO KNOW

Growing up, I had very little empathy.

Only cared about myself and my feelings.

But the tragic incident with Kholon aunt completely changed my outlook on life.

Individually, we are all just one pixel in the picture of life.

If we only care about our feelings, then we are doing ourselves a massive disservice.

I know I did not see Kholon aunt enough throughout the year to truly empathize with her depression.

But the lesson was not lost whatsoever.

The lesson that I picked up was that I needed to care for my fellow peers.

Not just care for my benefit.

But care to be a good human being.

ʜUMAN LIFE

Unfortunately we are not taught this in school enough.

But I truly do believe that empathy marks true intelligence.

Empathy gives you a peek into someone's internal world.

Empathy connects our hearts with one another.

It is the invisible bond that connects humanity.

It is time we begin to take empathy seriously.

CURIOSITY

Curiosity is the spark of empathy. You must be curious if you want to empathize.

'So be curious about others? Got it.'

Not so fast.

Listen carefully.

You cannot empathize efficiently if you do not know yourself yet.

You must first make the attempts to empathize with yourself.

Take some time to get to know those internal emotions that you are feeling.

Truly feel out your emotions. No running when you have strong feelings overwhelming you.

Feel & release.

Super scary at first, but if you stick with it you will feel 10x better.

While you have those negative emotions, take some time to analyze the thoughts that are running through your mind.

Analyze your body language.

Truly get to know yourself internally.

GOT IT?

'Yessir, I have spent a few weeks not running away from my emotions. I have been running towards them and I have much more clarity.'

Great.

Now you can make the most out of your empathy.

Take some time to keep in touch with your friends & family.

Anyone reading this is part of the level up tribe, so I know you guys do not have too much time on your hands.

You guys are busy leveling up different elements of your life.

But stop.

Remember this.

When we are on our deathbed, we are not going to just remember our work. We are going to remember our experiences with our loved ones.

So even if you are busy, make the time to stay in touch with everyone.

If someone is going through a rough patch in their life, give them your ear.

Even if it seems like a burden, do it anyways.

You're a winner, right?

'Yessir.'

Then carry yourself like a winner.

Kill it with your goals & kill it with your empathy.

LOSS OF A LIFE LEADS TO LESSONS

It is sad that my aunt's death is what it took for me to learn empathy.

Truly do wish I would have asked her what was wrong rather than thinking she was just having a bad day.

But there is no time for regrets.

Thank you Kholon aunt for the impact that you made on my life, I will never forget you.

Level up tribe, use my story as an example for your life.

Once you close this email, I want you all to be good humans.

Do not ONLY chase money. We have an abundance mentality. The money will come & go. Stack your paper, but do not revolve your life around it.

Let us be the special ones who reach out a helping hand to someone that needs it.

Let us be the ones who step up when someone is down.

We will redefine what it means to be successful.

Because it is not the size of our wallets that determine our worth.

It is the size of our compassion & willingness to give back to our community that determines our worth.

We will live up to our potential with flying colors.

We never settle in this side of the world.

Time to get to work.

The End

CHECK OUT THE OTHER BOOKS IN THE SERIES

ARMANITALKS  

www.ingramcontent.com/pod-product-compliance
Lightning Source LLC
Chambersburg PA
CBHW050313160726
48002CB00001B/14